CROSS OVER

Xenn Seah

CROSS OVER by Xenn Seah
Copyright© 2003

All scripture quotations are from the King James Version of the Holy Bible.

Cross Over
Modesto, CA, USA
E-mail: xennseah@gmail.com

Designed by Matthew Seah

Printed in USA
Fourth printing January, 2017

ISBN 1535028297

Introduction

Finally, the noise woke me up, but I lay there still groggy from sleep. Looking at the gap at the bottom of my bedroom door, I could see shadows moving up and down the floor outside. My first thought was that my mother was home, so I got up and opened the door. It was a mistake!

There were law enforcers in my apartment. My eyes flew wide open, and I slammed the door closed. As I fumbled to relock it, I didn't stand a chance. The four narcotics officers slammed their shoulders against the door on the other side, and I was knocked backward. They rushed in and threw me to the floor.

The next thing I knew I was sitting on the bed with my hands cuffed behind my back. I was now a desperate man. If they were to find out what I had in my room, I would be in more than just big trouble.

In that instant, knowing I was surely caught, I cried out, "Jesus, help me! Jesus, help me!" The words just rolled out of my mouth. That dying feeling was all over me, and I thought, "That's it, I need help." It was obvious to me that I needed something or someone bigger than I to help me out of this mess.

Xenn Seah

Dedication

I would like to dedicate this book to my mother who never gave up on me and was always willing to accept me back. No matter where I was or how low I had sunk, I always knew I had a home to return to. Your love in my life was ever constant. I love you, Mom!

To my wife, Barbara, for believing in the transforming power of Jesus Christ in my life. You have been so patient and understanding. Your love and encouragement have made it possible for me to write this book. I love you Barbie!

To my children, Scott and Erin, for being such sweethearts. You bring joy and laughter into my life. Your patience has allowed daddy to complete this book. I love you pumpkins!

To all the Chinese people I have come to know in the last year, you are my family. Thank you for allowing me to be a part of your lives.

Acknowledgements

Special thanks to Nathan Maki for writing the draft copy of this book. You provided the backbone for this book and gave it its flow. It would not have been possible without you.

I want to also express my heartfelt appreciation to the following people:

Barbara, my wife, for putting in many countless hours of editing the manuscript and offering sound advice.

Rev. Alonzo Dummitt, my pastor, for encouraging me and supporting me in the Chinese Ministry.

Lois Lazzara, for her typesetting and computer expertise.

Dr. Genny Miller, for showing me how to be a soul winner.

Laurie Nelson, for her editing skills and a sharp eye.

Rev. Lee Stoneking, for showing me how to be sensitive to the Spirit.

Rev. Anthony Tamel, for his Christian example and imparting to me his administrative and people skills.

Rev. Frank Tamel, for imparting to me his wisdom in counseling.

Barbara Willoughby, for her advice on putting a book together.

Rev. Steve Willoughby, for believing in me and being an example of an anointed preacher.

Contents

Foreword

Xenn Seah is the classic example of the total saving power of Jesus Christ.

What family was unable to do, what society found an impossibility, and what he could not accomplish as a man lost in the sea of life, Jesus came walking into his storm and pulled his sinking life from the depths!

In every generation, there are those that are rescued from the destructive forces of death and hell to show forth the praises of Him who is ALL powerful! He has received that rescuing touch from the Master's Hand, and the world must concede that Jesus is still the Master of the storm.

This book, written from the heart of the man rescued, will bless you and confirm all over again that God and His Word are the most powerful help on planet earth.

A man armed with the knowledge of the Bible has the ability to help mankind more than anyone else in the world today. Xenn is one of those men, and I recommend not only his testimony to you but his life and ministry as well.

May you be blessed and reminded of the unseen hands ever reaching for the likes of all of us as you read these pages.

Rev. Lee Stoneking
Author and Evangelist

Foreword

It took a "magnificent" Christ to miraculously lift Xenn Seah out of his miserable existence as a hopeless drug addict in Singapore and use him for God's glory.

I met Xenn in Singapore shortly after his surrender to the sovereignty of Christ. I didn't know him prior to his encounter with Christ, and on that, I have little comment.

However, the change wrought in him after he received the infilling of God's Spirit didn't take his tender, non-confrontational spirit away from him, but it gave him the desire to be a bold witness for Jesus Christ.

Since then, he has been blessed with a beautiful wife and two wonderful children and most important of all, he finds himself in the middle of a harvest field of thousands of Chinese that have migrated to Ottawa, Ontario, Canada, with the hope of a better life. Under Xenn's ministry, many will come to experience the love of God and be blessed with the unsearchable riches that are in Christ.

Bishop Frank Tamel

1

BREAK-IN

The break-in began as innocently as any break-in can: three little boys breaking into their own school. Chain link rattled as my two friends and I clambered over the six-foot fence surrounding the building. There we were, standing inside the fence in broad daylight, a trio of obvious amateurs. The concrete face of our school loomed ten stories above us. While one friend dashed towards the fishpond a few meters away, I spread out with my other friend, scanning the grounds for any sign of life. His mission was to scoop a single goldfish out of the water and get out of there fast.

Everyone was on holiday from school, so nothing moved in the schoolyard. There wasn't a sound. I was excited, getting an adrenaline rush that comes from doing something sneaky. Besides, we meant no harm; we were just doing it for fun. In our minds, we were innocent.

I really didn't think anything of it. I'd been stealing little things here and there since I was small. Being poor all my young life, I had long ago decided that if I was ever going to have things, I'd just have to steal them. I definitely couldn't afford anything and neither could my parents, so I had gotten used to just taking what I wanted.

Suddenly, as my friend scooped the goldfish, a security guard appeared around the corner of the building. We were shocked to see he had only one arm. We yelled to our friend, "Guard! Run!" Spotting us, the guard waved that one arm and shouted for us to stop. Of course, we ran. In the moment, there was no time for fear. The three of us made a mad dash for the fence while the guard followed us at a dead run. The fence, that had seemed so easy to climb over, now loomed high over us like a prison wall. We scrambled up, and I, being the lightest of the three, made it over the quickest. My older, heavier friend with the goldfish was not so lucky.

"I've got you now," shouted the guard, as he grabbed him by the shirt-tail with his one good hand. He pulled him down, muscled him to the ground, and twisted his arm up behind his back. This was all I saw over my shoulder before I lost myself in the dirty streets and narrow alleys of our less-than-prosperous district of Singapore.

By the time I neared home, I was much calmer. That post-adrenaline rush had set in, and I thought it was a rather good prank for the day. There were no foreseeable consequences, and I was home free! I walked up our street and turned into the alleyway that led to the house my family shared with twenty-three other families. I passed between the rows of smaller, cheaper little hovels that lined the alleyway, passed the common kitchen, and escaped into the main house.

Little did I know, that as I safely sat at home, my less fortunate friend sat in the interrogation room in the nearby police station with tears in his eyes. He screamed as the police officer brought the metal spoon down, once more, on his cut and bleeding knuckles.

The inspector leaned in close. "Who else was with you? Give us their names!" My friend shook his head, and the spoon smashed down again, bringing another scream, "Tell me!"

Finally, he could take no more. In a choked voice, he gave them our two names. The inspector left the room and dispatched a police cruiser.

I was still lying on the floor, smiling secretly to myself, when there was a knock on the door. My mother opened it, and two policemen filled the doorway, pushing their way inside. It was impossible for me to hide in our tiny little room. There was no time and no place. Their narrowed eyes scanned the whole room in a second, and then they fingered me, "You! Let's go."

My mother instantly leaped to my defense. "Why? What has he done?"

"I'm afraid he was stealing from the school. He's going to have to come with us."

Just as quickly, my mother turned on me with anger flushing her face. "You're stealing already? Your life is ruined!"

What would she have thought if she knew how long I had already been stealing?

The police took me by the arms and hustled me towards the door. My grandmother, always prone to spoiling me, followed along behind gesturing and pleading with the officers. "He's just a little boy, it's nothing! Look how scared he is. It was nothing!"

It was as though they didn't hear her. They marched me through the halls, down the staircase, and out the door. I was hoisted so high that instead of walking I was doing a quick dance on tiptoes. Their grip on my arms was brutally tight. All of a sudden, the innocent prank didn't seem like so much fun anymore. Neighbors looked curiously out of their doors and windows, and I could hear their whispers. "Thief!" "Police station!" "So young!" All my cockiness and self-satisfaction was gone. I just felt fear. My mother and grandmother came out of the house behind us, watching as I was locked into the back seat of the police car, and we pulled away. They followed us on foot as we drove the two blocks to the station.

My family and I had no chance to talk. The police marched me inside to the reception desk, and we were redirected upstairs to the interrogation room. There they seated me roughly in a straight-backed wooden chair and left as the inspector entered.

He paced back and forth appearing not to see me. I kept my eyes glued to the grains of the wood floor. Then, he stopped right in front of me and leaned down. His thin slanted eyes were locked onto mine. "So you're the ingenious mastermind, are you? Your two friends told me all about you." He paused and waited for my response, but I kept my mouth shut. He continued, "You're in a lot of trouble you know? It would be better if you just confessed and told us everything. It will go easier for you."

Somehow, in my childish wisdom, I knew better than to admit to anything. No one had to tell me to keep quiet to avoid incriminating myself. That's just something kids know instinctively. I didn't realize that he was trying to manipulate me, or that my friends really hadn't said I was the mastermind. I just knew that admitting to anything was a sure way not to get out of the jam I was in.

Finally, they decided to lock us up for the night and release us in the morning. Walking down the hall, along rows of cells, the stench of stale urine and the unwashed bodies of previous occupants assaulted my senses. They thrust me into a cell, and I stumbled and fell. As I picked myself up, I looked around and took in my surroundings. The place was depressing – bare brick walls and a bare floor, not a stick of furniture anywhere, not even a straw mat to sleep on. The only object in the room was a spittoon in the corner – my washroom. I was alone. Alone, except for the bugs. Bed bugs! They were my constant companions through the night as I curled up in a ball in the corner and tried to sleep.

As it happened, I had picked the right friends to be caught with. One of them had a well-to-do father who happened to know the police chief. The other, the one who was caught in the schoolyard, had an uncle who was a police inspector. Thanks to their connections, we were out of prison the next day. In spite of a night spent in that awful cell, I left the station with the confident impression that stealing wasn't really such a big deal after all. We'd been let off with just a stern warning and a night in jail. Already, I was starting to grow numb to the seriousness and possible consequences of crime.

CROSS OVER

The year was 1967. I was nine years old. My friends would go on to attend the best schools and become successful in life. My destiny was to be far different.

2

GANG RECRUITING

When I woke up in our tiny room soon after my release, I felt a strange sensation as I began to recall that something significant had taken place. It's not as if I'd forgotten, but sleep had pushed it to the back of my mind. Now that I was alert, the memory burst to the forefront in vivid color, and I relived the whole terrible experience. It felt so strange to hear my mother calling me, scolding me for sleeping in, and telling me that I'd be late for school if I didn't get up. Whenever you go through an experience like I had, you somehow expect it to change your life. Yet here I was, getting ready for a typical day.

Like the majority of Chinese families in Singapore, my family was Buddhist. Like all Buddhist homes, we had an altar where we burned joss sticks and offered up prayers to a variety of gods, idols, and ancestors. The smell of the incense and the sounds of the chanting prayers were a comforting presence. My mother was constantly praying and offering alms for safety, favor, and blessings for her children. Little did I know at the time, but Buddha did not have ears to hear or eyes to see. As my path started to become more and more wayward, my mother would put more and more time and energy into praying at this idolatrous altar. Sad to say, it was all for naught.

The house where I lived with my mother, father, grandmother, and sisters was unbelievably crowded. Each family had little more than a twelve-foot square room for total living space because the landlord had subdivided the house into twenty-four tiny cubbyholes to draw as much rental money as he could. The result was ninety-five people, about sixty adults and thirty-five children, jammed into every nook and cranny. Like most people in Singapore in the sixties, our parents were engrossed in working long hours in a desperate attempt to make ends meet. They were simply trying to maintain a minimum standard of living. With parents so preoccupied, the children were pretty much left to their own devices. Generally, that meant we ran riot.

Still wearing pajamas, I ran down the halls and stairways to the alleyway in front of the house. Already, the open space was crowded and bustling with street vendors preparing for their day. An old Indian man was making *meesiam*, a type of rice noodle with curry gravy. He held a long stirring stick. Sometimes he used it to stir his huge wok of noodles which was at least five feet across, and sometimes he used it to menace children who came too near to smell the delicious scents. As soon as he was finished, he would push his cart into the streets to sell a plate of curry noodles with half an egg and a few cubes of tofu for twenty-five cents. We were rather proud to have him in our neighborhood. He was one of the most famous curry noodle vendors in Singapore.

Among the noise and competing smells of the alleyway, I joined the other thirty-four children who lived in the same house with me. There we lined up, each with our mug of water and toothbrush, scrubbing away at our teeth as if we were in a race to see who could wear the enamel off the fastest. Then dipping up the water that was left in my mug with a little rag, I wiped it over my face, and I was ready for school.

I walked to school in the early morning light. Singapore was already awake and bustling. Shopkeepers were taking down the eight-foot planks that blocked the doors of the shops that lined the winding streets. Out front, others swept the dirty street with rough straw brooms. This was a rather hopeless effort, like trying to sweep a dirt floor free of dirt. With their apartments above their shops, these shopkeepers lived in a small circle, constantly working to eke out a living. They were the lucky ones.

The streets were full of those who weren't fortunate enough to have proper living quarters or a stable workplace. As I made my way down the streets, I thought nothing of seeing prostitutes still on the street corners after an unfruitful night or the desperate beggars that lurked in alleys and squatted in doorways.

Singapore in the sixties was far from the beautiful, prosperous metropolis it is today. This was long before former Prime Minister Lee Kuan Yew's reforms transformed Singapore into the ninth most prosperous nation in the world. Instead of the soaring, graceful skyscrapers that now form the skyline, there were grass-roofed hovels and crowded tenements. I remember drawing our washing water from the same sluggish river where we dumped our washroom waste. My wife once commented that her immigrant grandparents didn't even live in such desperate conditions way back when they first came to Canada. But this was my world; it was all I knew. And therefore, barely noticing my surroundings, I just walked on to school.

Our school was a mixed public school in a less than desirable district where drugs and gangs were common. As I made my way through the gate and into the schoolyard, I felt a little shiver. Looking down the fence, I could see the place where we climbed over just the week before and the small fishpond where my unfortunate friend had scooped up his tiny golden prize. It seemed strange to act so normally now and to go to class as if nothing had happened. At break time, as load after load of children poured out of the big elevator onto the playground, I stood to the side, looking around at my surroundings. I was sure that the other children and all of the teachers were looking at me. Did they know? Here, a group of students clustered together laughing. At me? There, a couple of teachers stood talking seriously and looking in my direction. I imagined they were discussing my dark future.

Suddenly, I was shaken from my thoughts by a hand gripping my shoulder and spinning me around. I was looking at pajama-clad legs. Looking up, I could see a sinewy chest above a muscular stomach, and by tilting my head way back, I could see Jiang's narrow face. He was a member of the

"18's", a gang that had already been trying to recruit me. (In Singapore, gang names are numbers instead of the colorful names like "Hell's Angels" so well known in Western society.) Luckily for me, he was smiling. "Xenn, big guy! I heard about your little escapade the other day. Sounds like good training for when you join our gang."

Still leaning my head back sharply, I replied, "You know I don't want to be part of a gang, Jiang. It's too dangerous for me."

He continued to grip my shoulder, and I tried to shrug it off. He just tightened his hold. "It's not dangerous. If you join us, we'll protect you. If you get in trouble, we'll settle it for you. If anybody has a beef with you, we'll just go for a table-talk and work things out."

As much as Jiang tried to convince me that the gang's life was safe, I knew differently. I'd seen this kind of "table-talk" before. It consisted of two rival gangs getting together for a meeting. They were usually armed to the teeth with knives, hooks and weapons of all kinds; and if the talks crashed, so would the gangs. The fighting could be vicious. Besides, gang members had to fulfill responsibilities and pay protection fees. I wanted no part of that.

Still, I didn't want to get Jiang and his gang mad at me, so I replied, "How 'bout if I just hang out with you guys for a bit right now and then decide, OK?"

Luckily for me, he didn't push it any further. He knew I was young and that they stood a good chance of reeling me in slowly. He finally eased his grip and patted me on my shoulder. "OK, Xenn, you're cool with us big guys. I know we can trust you, right?" I just nodded. "So you can be our lookout, OK? I nodded again, feeling fear and excitement twist around each other in my stomach. He smacked me on the shoulder again, saying, "Come around anytime," and then he swaggered off. I saw him join up with a couple of other teens by the fence. They stopped and talked for a minute and then walked away together. With my stomach in knots, I stood there until the teachers called us back inside. For some strange reason, I had a hard time concentrating on schoolwork that afternoon.

3

TABLE-TALK

I got the message in the usual way; a whispered word in my ear in the schoolyard, a time and a place, and no more. There would be a beating tonight, and I would be the lookout. I had done this many times before and knew the drill, but still, my nerves were tense.

Sitting at home in our room, leaning up against the pile of battered suitcases that held our clothes, I wondered what tonight's target had done. Maybe he was a lone drug dealer cutting in on their turf, or a member of a rival gang, or maybe just a prospective recruit that had refused to pay the protection money – like me. Needless to say, conflicting emotions filled my mind as I sat there, waiting. Time seemed to crawl. I got up and paced the few steps to the window and back, pausing each time to look out. Our room was in the back of the building, so our window looked down on the back alleyway and across at the tenement behind us. Seeing nothing there to hold my attention, I started to pace back and forth again. Outside, I could hear the other kids running around, shouting and laughing, but I was in no mood to join them. My thoughts were too dark and troubled.

I went through the rest of the day keeping to my routine, staying quiet and waiting for nightfall. Finally, we all laid down, and I pretended to sleep until I heard everyone's breathing become regular.

It wasn't the most comforting place to lie quietly. Once, a spider the size of a dinner plate dropped onto my chest from the ceiling above while I was trying to go to sleep. He was as scared as I was. He leaped away and scurried out of sight through the huge cracks in the wall. Now, as I waited, my eyes searched the dark corners above, and I wondered if that monster still lurked about.

Someone started to snore softly. Still, I didn't move. It felt like an hour had passed before I dared to stir. Getting up as quietly as possible, I slipped out of the room. The house was old, and every footstep brought a squeak of protest from the floorboards. With my senses heightened, each squeak sounded like it should have been loud enough to wake everyone in the building, but they slept on, soundly.

Easing open the door, I looked around and then quietly sprinted the fifty feet down the alleyway to the street. I paused to look around one more time. What had seemed so innocent in daylight, was ominous and threatening in the darkness. There were desperate people on the streets. Shadow melded with shadow, moving along the sides of buildings, down narrow streets, clustering here and there, meeting and parting. In this dark world, I became just another shadow flitting silently to the meeting place.

My eyes had adjusted by the time I arrived, and I could make out the milling shapes of my gang members in the dark. I called softly, and they replied. I joined up with them, and after a few whispered instructions, we set out. I learned that we were after a member of another gang who had been putting the moves on one of our guy's girlfriends. According to the plan, they would find him in his house, drag him down to the alleyway outside, and lay on the beating while I watched the street out front.

With nerves strung tight, I crouched in the darkness and scanned the street for any sign of the police, the victim's parents, or the rival gang. I heard a muffled shout from inside the building. The sound was cut off quickly, and I knew they had stuffed his mouth full of cloth. They dragged the victim down the stairs, and I caught a quick impression of bodies and raised clubs as they rushed him around the corner. The darkness of the alley swallowed them up, and they disappeared out of sight.

My eyes flicked back and forth and up and down the street, searching every shadow, every doorway, and every corner. I scanned the buildings, expecting lights to come on at any minute. My ears were alerted to every sound, listening for running feet, shouts, or sirens. But the only sounds I could hear were of the beating: grunts of effort and the thud of wood and fist on flesh. My stomach turned, and my teeth clenched. Finally, I heard the whispered order, "Dump him," and then the soft slapping of sandals on the street coming toward me. One of them patted me on the shoulder and said, "Good job." Everything ended as quickly as it had begun and I was left to find my way home in the darkness.

The gang leader of the man the "18's" had busted up, sent word and arranged for a table-talk to resolve this issue before it turned into a full-fledged war. Again, I kept watch from the doorway of a coffee shop as the two rival gangs filed in. The leaders of both gangs and their seconds were unarmed. Everyone else was far from unarmed. They sported machetes, which we called *parangs,* sharply honed axes, knives, hooks, and clubs. As soon as they walked in, the customers scrambled to exit, crashing tables and chairs as they ran past me.

I was supposed to keep watch for police outside. Instead, I wanted to see the action inside. The two gang leaders and their seconds advanced to a table that had been cleared in the middle of the room. All around, and behind each of them, their respective gang members lounged in booths, straddled chairs, and leaned against walls. They were a rough crew and heavily tattooed to show their loyalty to their gang. Some had long greasy hair. Most wore the tight jeans that were so popular at the time. Some seemed almost sleepy, leaning back with half-closed eyes. Others were on edge, leaning forward to hear the progression of the talks.

From my vantage point outside, I couldn't hear what they were saying, but I could see the leaders arguing. As they got more heated, their shouts reached my ear. The leader of the other gang was yelling, "You almost killed my man! Now, what are you going to do about that? You had no right!"

"No right? Don't talk to me about rights," the leader of the "18's" retorted. "I saw him with my girl! He had it coming!"

"Listen, you owe us something for our man being broken up like that. Otherwise, there can be no peace between us. Now! What will you give us?"

"Give you? I'll give you this." The leader of the "18's" was working himself into a cold fury. He rose and jabbed a stiff finger at the other leader. His voice was tight and hard as he said, "I'll give you one chance to walk away from this whole situation, alive. You walk away and let this go. He got what was coming to him. If you don't like it, we can do the same for you!"

The opposing leader shoved the table and leaped to his feet as he shouted, "It's more war then!"

All of a sudden, clubs whistled through the air, and he and his second reached up, snatched the weapons, and were armed. The two sides sprang into action. They roared as they vaulted wildly over chairs and tables. Even from outside, I heard the impact as they crashed together. I heard the meaty sound of clubs making contact, the clanging of *parangs,* the clashing of knives, the shouts, and the screams. Inside, all I could see was a mass of bodies, swinging arms, and glinting weapons. I heard smashing glass and cracking wood as they wrecked the coffee shop in their fury. There was no order and no battle lines, just deadly chaos. One of the gang members dashed out the door, streaming blood. He was clutching the hilt of a knife that was sticking out of his belly. I learned later that another went home with seventeen stab wounds. He made it to the hospital, and somehow, incredibly, survived.

Suddenly, over the sounds of the fighting, I heard several sirens coming our way. The proprietor, cowering in the back room, had called the police. Leaning inside the door, I screamed, "POLICE! RUN!" Then taking my own advice, I ran myself.

The two gangs broke apart and limped away. They were supporting each other and nursing wounds as they tried to stop the flow of blood. All that was left was a scene of total devastation. Overturned tables, smashed dishes, and broken chairs littered the floor. Everything was bathed in eerie red blood. The whole scene is still in my head. A memory so traumatic never goes away. Such were the days of my youth.

4

MY FRIENDLY NEIGHBORHOOD DRUG DEALER

Fighting in the streets was only one part of my childhood education. I was taught well at home too. My parents never intended to steer me wrong, but the whole atmosphere in the house was unhealthy. Every evening, one of the mothers in our building would get all decked out and go to work. She was a prostitute. Every morning, she would come home and crash, as her children fended for themselves. She would never know whether they ate breakfast or not, or even if they went to school or not. In such cramped, close conditions, there were few secrets. What few things the thin walls could conceal, we kids were still sure to find out.

It was common knowledge that there were homosexual dealings going on. You could see men coming and going all the time. An Indian man, two rooms down from us, had a Chinese stepson. Often, in the mornings, we would see the Chinese boy come out of the room crying and beaten. Curious, I asked my grandmother what was wrong with him. Why was he always crying? She would get very serious and quiet and told me not to bother myself about what our neighbors were doing. We were to keep to ourselves. It seemed impossible to ignore, though. The wall between our rooms was far from soundproof. Of course, my friends and I were not satisfied to leave well enough alone. So one morning, when the man in the middle room was away, we slipped in. The sight we saw through the cracked, knot-holed plank walls was beyond our imagination – too awful to describe.

And then there were the drug dealers. One day, a big truck pulled up at the end of the alley leading to our house. A large, muscular Indian man jumped out and looked around. He sported a big potbelly, a thick black mustache, and tattoos across his upper arms and chest.

He slowly scanned up and down the street. Seemingly satisfied, he climbed up into the back of the truck and reappeared with a bulging, brown gunnysack. Curiously, a few of us kids tagged along behind him as he thumped up the stairs and down the hall under his heavy load.

From the beginning, he seemed to favor me. Pointing to me in the gaggle of kids, he called me over, asking, "You want to make a dollar?" What kind of a question was that? A dollar then was like ten bucks now! So, as the rest of the children watched jealously, I helped him tote his few belongings from the truck to his room. Sure enough, he gave me the dollar as promised. This would buy four plates of curry noodles with egg and tofu! What a prize!

As time went by, we noticed that there was a lot of traffic in and out of the Indian man's room. People were always coming and going. One day, I hung around the door after a man went in, hoping to catch a quick glimpse of what was going on as he left. Spotting a little knothole, I bent over to peep in.

All of a sudden, the door was flung wide open, and I was staring at the Indian man's wide belly as it filled the doorway. Caught off guard, I tried to run, but he grabbed me by the back of my T-shirt with one big hand. Reeling me in laughing, he said, "If you want to see what's going on so bad, little friend, why don't you just knock and come in?" To my astonishment, he ushered me into his room. I felt excited and a little scared, as though I was entering a forbidden place.

He closed the door behind us and threw the double locks. While I looked around the room with wonder, my eyes passed quickly over the sparse furnishings. I took in the low cot, the side table, and the old lamp. I then focused on the table and stools in the corner. Another man was already sitting there. Seeing my interest, the Indian man led me over to the corner, warning "Look only, no touch." On one side of the table was a small stack of four-inch square papers and also a long row of what looked like paper sausages. On the other side were a small set of scales and a tray of small plastic tubes.

As I watched, the man on the stool dipped into the big gunnysack beside him and pulled out a small handful of what looked like old dead weed. With his other hand, he shaped one of the papers into a half-circle scoop and poured the weeds into it. He deftly rolled it all together, licked the paper's edge, and folded in the ends to make another neat little sausage.

My new friend pointed to the gunnysack and asked, "You know what's in there?" I shook my head emphatically. He gave a short chuckle. "And what about that?" he asked, pointing to the bags and tubes of white powder. I shook my head again, and he laughed again. Somehow, I felt ashamed like I should know this, but he calmed my fears right away saying, "It's OK kid, even the cops don't know what this stuff is yet, no worries. But they soon will, and so will you."

The big man then proceeded to give me a crash course in marijuana and heroin. Little did I know then, how well I would become acquainted with this stuff in the years to come. If only I would have run the other way – if only. What pain, what sorrow I could have avoided.

I was already familiar with the idea of drugs but only the traditional Singapore ones like morphine and opium. When I was only five years old, my grandfather brought me to an opium den with him, and I watched him suck the pipe in the smoky, dark room. What I was seeing now, however, was something new!

Did I ever have a story to tell my friends! To have entered the sanctum and return alive to recount the tale was quite a feat. But I was not content with just a story, so when my friend invited me in again I readily accepted. He took one of the little rolls from the table, cut a piece off the end, and gave it to me. I eagerly accepted it as he stuck the other part in his mouth. We lit these rolls and breathed in the strange aroma. My head seemed to float up off my body, spinning around and around as it ascended. The rest of my body joined it in weightlessness, and I was gone. This was my introduction to a long hard road.

Before I knew it, I was sampling drugs here and there, then more and more regularly. My Indian friend gave me free samples for doing little errands for him: dropping off a tube here or a roll there, handing out the drugs and taking in the money at the door when he was busy. Sometimes, he would give me a dollar or two as a reward, and before I knew it I was a runner. With his free samples, my friend was trying to make me dependent on him so that I would work for him in exchange for my daily ration. Before long, I was smoking marijuana almost every day. I was high half the time. It turned out that the Indian man was right when he said I would learn all about the new drugs. My education in that field was destined to follow a very progressive course.

5

CLOSE CALLS

As it turned out, the Indian man was also right about the cops not being familiar with the new drugs. Singapore's traditional drugs were opium and morphine. These had been imported as early as the forties and fifties. However, in the seventies, with the coming of the hippie generation in the United States also came the rising popularity of heroin and marijuana. American sailors imported the new drugs into Singapore, but the police hadn't quite caught up with the new trend yet.

The day I put my friend's words to the test began like many others. I knocked on his door and called in. Recognizing my voice, he opened the door for me with his habitual smile. "Today should be an easy one for you; just one quick run." By now, it was second nature to get his brief instructions, pocket the drugs and set out for the rendezvous point to meet his customer.

Halfway there, I ran into trouble. As I walked down the dirty sidewalk, I wove my way through the traffic of food vendors with their carts full of tasty morsels, and shoppers arguing and bargaining loudly with shopkeepers. This felt good. I felt hidden and unobtrusive.

Suddenly, I saw them. The police were sweeping down the road in my direction. I ran! It didn't matter that they were just doing a random spot-check. Just the chance that they would stop me was enough to send me scurrying in the opposite direction. Behind me, I heard a shout as I ducked into a narrow alleyway. Ahead of me was a corner, a sharp turn, and a dead end. Staring hopelessly at the sheer brick walls rearing up around me, I backed into a corner and waited. It didn't take long for the three police officers to see me cowering. They surrounded me and forced me to spread-eagle against the wall. They patted me down and emptied my pockets.

One of them found the small tubes I carried, packed an inch deep with heroin. Forcing my face sideways against the rough brick, he held one up in front of my eyes so close I went cross-eyed trying to focus on it. My only glimmer of hope came when he asked, "What is this?" He actually seemed not to know. Remembering what the drug dealer had told me, I decided to chance it. My mouth half crushed against the wall, I gasped, "It's just medicine, just medicine." Miraculously, they believed me and released me. Still shaking, I finished my run and reported back. The Indian man just laughed when I told him the story. "See? I told you so," he said.

And so it continued, relatively uneventfully. I ran drugs for him; he supplied me with the drugs that I came to use every day. Then one day, my drug-dealing friend simply disappeared. Looking in the knothole in the door at his bare room, I fondly remembered our first meeting when I ended up staring stupidly at his gut as he opened the door. I liked to think he may have returned home to Malaysia, but who knows? Why would he just leave without a word? However, drug dealing was a dangerous and desperate business, so I shouldn't have been surprised. One way or the other I was never to see him again.

That left me with the serious problem of a supplier for what had fast become a constant drug habit. By this time, I was totally addicted. I had to have my drugs regularly to avoid withdrawals. I had dropped out of school and was working in common labor jobs, construction jobs, and contract work to support my drug addiction. My friends and I lived on drinking, drugs and, disco. It was a wild life.

Besides the disco clubs, our other favorite hangout was the coffeehouse. We enjoyed the coffee, milkshakes, and soft drinks almost as much as the drinks and drugs of the clubs. Although the music was a bit calmer than what was playing in the clubs, the change of pace now and then was welcoming.

One night, some buddies and I were kicking back in one of the booths with our drinks. We were enjoying the music and chatting when the door flew open and several narcotics officers entered. Scanning the room, they quickly picked the six of us out of the crowd. With our long hair and bad attitudes, we looked like hooligans. Coming straight over, one of the officers demanded, "All right, on your feet and outside. We're checking you over. Move it!"

I rose. Every muscle was tense. I knew I was the only one in this group that did drugs, and I had some on me. As they hustled us in a group toward the door, I desperately reached into my pocket and tossed the tube of heroin sideways into a booth. None of the officers seemed to have noticed, and I breathed a sigh of relief. The tension was draining, but my relief was short-lived. As they lined us up against the wall outside, they began frisking us and emptying our pockets.

The door opened behind us, and a young couple came out holding the tube of white powder. "Officer, one of them tried to dump this in the coffeehouse. We saw him toss it into one of the booths." Cursing them inwardly, I could only stand there, rigid in fear of giving myself away with the slightest movement.

"Which one of them was it?" the officer asked.

"We couldn't see clearly because his back was to us." He paused, and I held my breath.

Then his girlfriend cut in eagerly, "I saw him. He had long hair and a green shirt." Somehow, I kept myself from looking down. I knew I was wearing my green shirt.

Glancing down the line of us, the officer pointed to me, and I stepped forward. I resigned myself to the consequences. But wait! The officer fingered another of my friends, and I glanced over quickly. He was wearing green, too! If it came down to it, I knew I wouldn't let him take the fall for me. I decided that, for now, I'd ride it out and see what happened.

"OK," the officer barked, "we'll take them all down to the station. Load them up." They hustled us away, loaded us into a police van, and headed off to the station. The station happened to be the same one I had been to years earlier – it was something far worse than goldfish theft this time. I got a strange sense of déjà vu as I was interrogated in the same room, led down the same hallway, and thrust into the same filthy cell. Even the stench was the same, or maybe it was worse. It was as if the cell had remained unwashed for the seven years since I'd last occupied it, and the smell had intensified. Just as before, I spent all night huddled on the bare stone floor, leaning up against the dreary brick wall, swatting and scratching at the bed bugs crawling over me.

Luckily for me, the result of my second stay was the same as the first. At the time, they had yet to develop a method of drug testing, so they couldn't confirm if I had been using drugs or not. Once again, I had picked my friends well; the father of the friend I was arrested with knew one of the inspectors in that station. The next morning, we were released and, I was back on the street with a fresh conviction that I was invincible, above the law.

One day, my world of freedom and wild parties came to an abrupt halt. I was conscripted. It is the duty of every Singaporean male to serve a mandatory two-year term in the National Service. I was recruited at eighteen years old and was sent for three months of basic military training. In no way was I ready for duty! The very thought was the biggest joke.

6

RECRUIT

"All right! Get up! Everybody up! I want all you sissies on the parade square by 0530 hours! You've got half an hour. Up!" I rolled over in my narrow military bed and groaned. My sergeant stood in the doorway of the barrack barking out his orders just like he did every morning. Why did he have to yell so loud? My head already hurt enough. All around me, the other trainees tumbled out of bed, dressing and rushing outside to form up for morning exercise.

I couldn't move. After making a concerted effort to swing my legs out of bed and failing miserably, I gave up and closed my eyes again. As a rule, drug addicts just aren't morning people. In what seemed like seconds later, the drill sergeant wrenched my blanket off, lifted me out of bed by my T-shirt and the back of my shorts, and threw me towards the door. He hissed in my ear, "Get out there and form up! Do you think you're in the army to sleep your life away?"

Every morning, we were to do our basic exercises. We started off with star jumps. After the first five minutes of this, I was out of breath. By the time we finished five minutes later, I was thoroughly miserable. By the time we finished ten minutes of frog jumps, I wished I were dead. Then we started into the sit-ups. With each contraction of my abdomen, I was sure I was going to retch. The feeling grew until it was just a constant sensation of nausea. When I tried to do my first pushup, I simply collapsed.

No amount of cussing or prodding by the drill sergeant could raise me from my spot facedown in the dirt. Finally, as everyone else finished, he got me to my feet and shoved me towards the jogging track. "Go! Go and do your run then! Pick it up!" I stumbled away.

I had the three-kilometer run down to a fine science. In a halfhearted run, I made it around the first turn. There, shielded from the eyes of my drill instructor, I dove into the bushes. I lay there miserable and exhausted in the undergrowth while my fellow trainees finished their first two laps. When they came around the third time I emerged, brushed the dirt and leaves off, and ran behind them for the final lap. Even so, I felt a stabbing pain in my side growing worse and worse until finally, I slowed to a walk. I finished with my hand clutching my side. Wow! Could my country ever be proud of me!

My drill sergeant was a muscular man without a spare ounce of fat on his body. How I envied him! He came jogging over, and he didn't look happy. "What do you think this is, a three-kilometer hike instead of a three-kilometer run? Why can't you keep up the pace, Xenn? What's wrong with you?" I couldn't very well explain to him that drug addicts lose their stamina, become lethargic, and usually wake up sometime in the afternoon instead of five in the morning. So, I just mumbled the usual excuses and limped off. It was breakfast time.

That was just our pre-breakfast warm-up; after breakfast came the real training. We were all fitted out in full army combat uniform. Six pouches ran across the front of my belt; each holding two magazines of twenty rounds. A water bottle pouch was on the side and a bayonet in the back. Hand grenades were strung on webbing across my chest. On top of all that, I carried my M-16 machine gun as we ran through the obstacle course. We wriggled under barbwire, scaled walls, leaped over streams, and waded through mud. We had weapons drills and firing drills. We went over unit tactics and flanking movements. We dismantled our guns for cleaning and then reassembled them again. Long before training ended that night, I was ready to collapse.

Training finally did end but not our work. After wading through mud and squirming through dirt all day, my uniform was filthy. I spent the next hour up to my armpits in soap and water, scrubbing out the ingrained dirt and then hung them up to dry. Next, I had to prepare my parade uniform. While I waited for one of the two irons to become available, I polished my boots. Dabbing a gob of Kiwi polish out of the tin, I coated my right boot thoroughly, rubbed it evenly, and then buffed it with a circular motion. I smiled at the boot, shook my head, and began the process all over again. And again. And again. Finally, I smiled and kept on smiling. I could see my teeth reflected in the high gloss finish of the boot. One boot down, one to go! At last, it was my turn to use the iron and the starch. The starch was of utmost importance. Only when my shirt could literally stand up on its own was my job done. All of this conspired to keep me up until nearly two in the morning. In three hours I would be waking up for another day of the same.

Just because I was enlisted didn't mean I was about to give up drugs. I smuggled in a small supply of heroin on my very first day, and my friends would replenish my supply during weekend visits. During the last month of training, we were issued weekend passes to go home. Of course, then I was free to get what I wanted. Because of the drugs, however, I did very poorly in the training regime. I just couldn't keep up.

As the three months of basic training drew to a close, my anticipation mounted. I was counting the days until I would join the regular unit and finally relax or at least sleep a little more and exercise a little less.

On the last day of training, I was summoned before commanding officer. I'd been there many times before as they repeatedly questioned me, asking me why I could never keep up with the training. But this day was different. I walked into his office and saluted stiffly. He was a distinguished looking man with steel gray hair at his temples, every inch a military man.

Looking at me with dark, piercing eyes, he returned my salute, saying, "At ease." I stepped into a wider stance with my feet spread and hands clasped behind my back. As he sat down, he opened a folder on his desk. "I've noticed over the past three months that you've had a difficult time with your training." He paused as if waiting for my response and then continued, "However, I've decided to overlook that. You're being assigned to a special unit that is being formed. Over the next nine months, you will take advanced training to prepare for special reconnaissance missions deep into enemy territory. You will learn to operate weaponry, gather information, and relay that information back to HQ. Your battalion will be the first formed for this type of mission. You will lead the way. Congratulations. That is all."

Far from feeling elation, I was in despair. I was sure that another nine months of training would kill me. During the next nine months, I took many different courses training for weapons ranging from pistols and small arms to 84mm bazookas and 120mm artillery. They wanted us to know how to use any enemy weapon we might capture. I learned about armor operation and movements, assault tactics, intelligence gathering, and withstanding torture. Through it all, I knew I was just a guinea pig. My job was to go behind the enemy lines and send information back to the HQ. Alone! No one needed to tell me that it was a dangerous proposition.

As it turned out, I was not bound for the enemy lines. I was bound for prison.

7

BUSTED

"So, look who's the big bad military man now!" my friend exclaimed. He danced forward with fists raised in mock fighting stance. "Come on, show me whatcha got," he taunted.

I just laughed, "If I showed you, it'd be the last thing you ever saw. Now shut up and let's go party!" We met up with another buddy on our way to my friend's house. I had a couple straws of heroin in my pockets and I was ready for a good time. As we walked down the street laughing and joking, I was feeling good. Life was fine – in my world anyway.

They seemed to come out of nowhere, sweeping towards us in the darkness like ghosts until they were almost on top of us – twelve narcotics officers. This time, I had no chance to run. I just stood staring while they surrounded the three of us. As they searched our pockets, my friends protested that they had nothing. I didn't bother to say a word. I was the only one in the group who did drugs. Inevitably, one officer found me out, and it was over.

This time I wasn't getting off with a one night stay in prison. They transferred me back to military headquarters where I was locked in a detention barrack. Staring at the stark gray cement wall, I wondered how long I would be in for. I was soon to find out. The door swung open, and two burly military police came in. They took me by the arms and hustled me out down the hall. For a moment, I felt like a nine-year-old kid again, trying to reach the floor between two police officers after stealing a goldfish.

The interrogating officer turned to face me as I entered the room. "Ah, Private Xenn, it seems you have been caught with possession. Now, why don't you tell me about yourself? How long have you been using drugs?" I just stared at him in silence. Possession was quite different from actual use. To answer him would be a de facto confession.

When he saw I wasn't going to answer, he continued, "I know you must have a source. Who supplies you with these drugs?" Once again, my mouth was shut so tight that my lips turned white. I wasn't about to squeal on my friends. Again and again, he probed me with questions. Asking, waiting in the silence and then asking again. His neck veins were popping. Finally, he lost patience. "Private, I've noticed that you stink. Put him in the shower!"

Before I knew it, the Military Police had me in the tiny white cubicle, handcuffed to the showerhead. The first blast of icy cold water hit me like a ton of bricks, forcing all air from my lungs. In agony, I twisted in the handcuffs and tried to avoid the pelting stream, but I only managed to expose different parts of my body to its flow. My teeth were chattering, and I was covered with goosebumps.

Suddenly, the water shut off, and I stood gasping and shaking.

The officer leaned against the shower doorway and calmly looked at me for a long moment. When he spoke, he was quiet, almost gentle. "Now that you're freshly showered and comfortable, maybe you're willing to be a little more accommodating." I cursed at him. My heart was burning with wrath, and hate streamed out from every pore.

He shook his head. "So hotheaded. You really need to cool down." They dragged me, still dripping from the shower, and handcuffed me back into my chair. The air conditioner in the room and the fan over my head clicked on and pumped cold air down onto my wet body. It was pure misery.

I found myself reaching into the dark recesses of my special training on withstanding torture. I used every trick and tactic that my spinning mind could remember to distance myself from the pain. Somehow, I managed to keep what was happening to my body from affecting my mind, and I refused to give in to the torture. Finally, they took my urine sample for testing and transported me from the military headquarters to a military prison.

By the time I got there, around midnight, my eyes were watering, and tears were rolling down my face. My nose was running, but with my hands handcuffed I couldn't wipe it dry. I could feel the cramps beginning in my gut, and I could tell I was going into full-fledged withdrawals. I thought I would rather be dead.

High metal gates swung slowly inward as we approached, and the vehicle pulled up in front of the main doors. When the back door opened, I caught a glimpse of high gray walls and blank barred windows before the MPs hurried me inside. The officers led me to a small, cold room. Things didn't look good. Two iron poles ran from floor to ceiling about five feet apart. They stretched my arms to each side, handcuffed a hand to each pole, and left me there shivering in the dark. As my stomach began to cramp up, I could no longer stand. I sunk to the cold bare floor and moaned. With my hands cuffed, there was nothing I could do when diarrhea set in. I spent the night in misery on the cement floor without a pillow or blanket, arms stretched to each pole, legs curled up to relieve the pressure on my gut.

At five the next morning, I was shaken awake and lifted to my feet. Unlocking the handcuffs, they dragged me, still half-asleep, outside to the exercise grounds. They pushed me into line with the other prisoners as an officer started yelling, "All right! I want fifty sit-ups. Now!"

In one big wave, the other prisoners dropped to the ground, lay back, and counted off in unison as they did their sit-ups. I sank to the ground, lay back, and moaned. As I clenched my stomach and attempted to force myself up, the only result was a stabbing pain in my gut. I lay back gasping. In my condition, so weakened by withdrawals, I couldn't even do a single sit-up. The MPs tried to get me up. They prodded me with their batons and kicked with their boots, but all I could manage to do was curl up in a ball and again wish I were dead. At the end of the day, I was taken back and spread between the poles again. This was the routine of my miserable life for the next ten days. I felt utterly helpless and hopeless. As far as I was concerned, this was hell on earth.

Afterward, I was put into a room with nineteen other prisoners. This was a vast improvement over my accommodations the night before. Every day was the same. We were up at 5 a.m. and allowed two minutes in the washroom. Imagine, trying to fit your morning routine into just two minutes. Fifteen minutes later, we had begun the exercises that would last all day; with only brief breaks for lunch and dinner. The military police treated us like animals, forcing us to do all sorts of demeaning things.

The test results from my urine sample were still pending. As yet, I had not been court-martialed, but I knew what the results would be. It was only a matter of time; not that it really mattered to me. Every waking moment was already a living nightmare. In my mind, it couldn't possibly get any worse.

The authorities were now becoming more sophisticated in detecting heroin use. My urine sample came back positive, and they now had all the evidence they needed to court-martial me. I was summoned before a tribunal and was sentenced to eighteen months in a military prison. By this time, the psychological withdrawals from drugs began. While the physical withdrawals could be over within a month or two, the psychological withdrawals could often last far longer and were torture in themselves.

On a morning just like every other, I woke up to a ringing bell and the shouts of guards. We lined up in our room and filed out to the washrooms for our two-minute allotment. Exercises then began.

Just as in the army, we did every kind of exercise possible. This jump, that jump, frog jump, star jump, sit-ups, push-ups, and running. An hour later, we broke for breakfast. Picking up my two pieces of bread, I tried to spread out the little dab of butter as far as possible. I ate it quickly, followed by a hard-boiled egg and a cup of diluted tea. Then we were back to exercises again.

We squared away into formation in the exercise yard, standing an arm's length apart, with eyes straight ahead. The officer barked, *Cepat! Jalan!* "Ready! March!" We swung into motion, chanting, *Kiri! Kanan! Kiri! Kanan!* "Left! Right! Left! Right!" in cadence, as we marched in unison. Finally, after an hour, we were given the command to break. Immediately, we dropped cross-legged to the ground and stared straight down. MPs paced the rows between us, twirling their baton canes. From down the row, I heard a sharp crack and a cry. One of the newcomers obviously didn't know enough not to raise his head to look around. I'd made the same mistake myself, but with the crack of the guard's cane on the back of my head and the dull, thudding headache that followed, I quickly learned my lesson.

After a while, I felt an ache in my neck from holding one position for so long. It spread slowly across my shoulders and down my back to my toes. It was thirty-four degrees Celsius outside, and the hard-packed ground we were sitting on felt like a skillet. Finally, we were given the order to stand. I stood, and my knees protested from being bent so long. The humidity was brutal, and we were weak.

Standing in our square again, the drill officer called out, "Left turn!" All together we pivoted left, raised one foot and stomped it down into place. "Left turn!" We turned again, repeating the procedure until we were facing back in the original direction.

As usual, we had lost the perfect lines of our formation, and the officer stormed at us, "You call that a line? You miserable bunch of misfits! Drop and count off fifty pushups!" As with everything we did, we had to be perfectly in time, holding our position after each pushup while calling out, "One, sir! Permission to continue, sir!" He gave the word and we continued, "Two, sir! Permission to continue, sir!" As the count rose, he would keep us longer and longer between pushups before giving us permission to continue. He seemed to enjoy the way our arms wobbled and shook. When we finally finished, we went back to regular exercises.

Suddenly, I heard my prison number being called. "Thirty-three!" I stepped out of the ranks, stomped once, gave a sharp salute, and barked, "Present, sir!"

"Prepare for boot drill, thirty-three!" My heart sank as I hurried to take off my boots. Boot drill was just another way of assigning impossible tasks and then punishing you for not being able to perform it to satisfaction. I knew they would give me ten seconds to put my boots back on and lace them tight – impossible. The officer called out, "Ready. Go!" In desperation, I tried to wrench on my boots and lace them up as he started counting, "One, Two, Three...." Today I was flying, though. I felt elated that maybe I would make it this once. At "Seven," I was just lacing up my second boot and pulling it tight, and then he ran through the last three numbers so quickly, the words blurred together. "Eight, Nine, Ten! Stop! Go sign up for an extra exercise." All this time, he was just mocking me!

Instead of going for lunch at 12 noon, I was put out on the sun-cooked parade square. They held this drill between 12 and 1 p.m. The sun was at its peak, and I would surely burn. This was their sadistic intention. I watched as they loaded a thirty-five-pound sandbag into a backpack. As I put my arms through the straps and pulled them tight, I could already feel the weight sitting heavy on my back and dragging my shoulders down. For the next hour, I sweat in the yard under the hot sun, marching, running, and jumping. The guards hurried and harried me, laughing at the way I blinked to clear the sweat from my stinging eyes.

Sometimes, under that kind of pressure, prisoners would argue with the guards or curse them, and that would earn them an extra thirty-five-pound pack to wear on their chest. I knew from harsh experience that complaints would only make it worse, so I kept quiet and endured.

Sweat soaked my T-shirt and shorts and rolled down my legs to my boots. The weight and chafing of the backpack spread a constant ache through my shoulders. Finally, after an eternity of dust and sun and heat, my extra exercise was over, and I could go for lunch.

I hurried to drink my thin soup and eat my mound of rice topped with a square of tofu and a few vegetables. They gave us five whole minutes to eat. We then had to wash our tray and hand it in for inspection.

The extra exercise was over, but now regular exercises continued until four in the evening. Finally, on command, we filed off the exercise square and to the showers. I jumped eagerly into the shower and reached for the tiny bar of soap. I just finished scrubbing my armpits, and then I was out of time. We were each given twenty seconds to wash – just enough to get ourselves wet. How ridiculous! Still filthy, I marched off to eat supper with the others.

Before we ate, we had to pray. Under the watchful eye of the commandant, we chanted together, "I thank the army for the good food. Without the good food, I go hungry. Permission to carry on, sir?" Not pleased with our unity and cadence he barked, *Semula!* "Over again!" We repeated it until he was satisfied, and finally, we dug in. Supper was tofu, soup, vegetables, and a piece of fat that may have had some meat on it. We had no choice but to eat it, fat and all.

Afterward, we were sent to our cells and locked up. The cell was tiny, maybe seven by ten feet. Six of us occupied this space. High overhead, a little barred window let in a bit of sunlight and fresh air. One inmate went to the washroom using the spittoon in the corner, and we groaned. "Man, now we're gonna have to sleep with that stench in here! Couldn't you hold it?"

We all laid down feet to feet on our miserable straw mats, exhausted from our strenuous day. One of my cellmates started to sing quietly. I just lay there and closed my eyes, daydreaming of a time when I would be out of prison and free of exercises, military police, and poor prison food. There was nothing to drink, nothing to read, and nothing to do. Sometimes, the inactivity could become as taxing as the exercises we were forced to do.

Around 7 p.m., the duty sergeant and the other guards came into the cellblock and over the loudspeaker they announced, "Cell parade! Prepare for inspection!" Instantly, the six of us sprang up and faced the wall in two lines of three. Our feet were spread shoulder width apart and hands were clasped behind our backs. We stood absolutely motionless. Silence blanketed the whole prison block, broken only by the slow measured pacing of the guards outside. No one was allowed to talk or move. We knew that the guards were randomly looking in through the peepholes in the doors. If we were caught moving or talking, we would all get extra exercises the next day, sometimes for up to two hours.

The door behind us opened, and down the line, we could hear the guards open other cells as well. "About face!" shouted the guard, and we pivoted together. There, through the doorway, we could see Sergeant Dan clenching his jaw and slamming his fist into his palm in his usual way. His large mustache twitched as he smiled a truly evil smile. "Good evening," he shouted. "Everyone ready for a blanket party?" I had expected as much.

On his order, the guards came in and stripped everything from the cell: the clothes that we wore, our slippers, our blankets, and our straw mats. They dumped everything in a heap in the hallway and continued down the line of open cells. This procedure was repeated until there was a small mountain of sixty men's personal belongings in the middle of the floor. At the sergeant's order, they mixed the pile thoroughly until it was impossible to keep track of our own belongings.

Then Sergeant Dan barked, "You have ten seconds to collect your things. Go!" He and the guards stood back as sixty men dove desperately onto the pile. We all knew that whatever we didn't collect, we would have to do without the next day. Pandemonium reigned in the hallway. Bodies hurtled together as we all threw ourselves on the pile. One of the first men there rose from the mass of inmates with a full armload of stuff scooped indiscriminately from the pile. Someone else tried to drag a pair of shorts away from him, and they fell to the ground together, rolling over and over in their struggle. Two cellmates had an impromptu tug of war over a ragged scrap of towel. There was an argument over whose sandals were whose, and it degenerated into a fight. Fists flew, shouts and cursing filled the air, and above it all, we could hear Sergeant Dan laughing at us.

With a whistle, they announced time up. We stood back, ragged; clutching what belongings we could, trying to figure out if they were indeed our own. The results were often comical. A hulking brute held a tiny pair of shorts. Another inmate struggled to put on two left sandals in different sizes. None of it, of course, was funny to us at the time.

From somewhere, Sergeant Dan had produced a beer bottle. He took a long swig, wiped the back of his hand across his mouth, and smiled that evil smile again. "Very nice, very nice," he chuckled. "Enjoying the party, aren't we? *Lagi-Lagi!* Do it again!" We dumped our belongings back in the center of the floor and waited for the word to hurl ourselves together again. This continued for an hour. Since we never knew when he would send us back to our cells, we had to play along with him each time or risk losing everything for a day.

Finally, around 10 p.m., by which time Sergeant Dan was drunk and laughing constantly, he let us go back to our cells. My cell hadn't done too badly. I was missing a sandal which I knew I would definitely miss the next day. We were short a couple of blankets and a T-shirt, but we had our sleeping mats, and at this point, sleep was all we were thinking about.

Even though we were only separated from the hard cement floor by a thin straw mat, sleep was not long in coming. We were exhausted. However, sleep was fitful at best because of the bed bugs. In the wee hours of the morning, they would come out and crawl all over us. They easily found their way into my ears and up my nostrils.

And so it continued, day after day. Our guards held complete power over us. We were totally subjected to their whims. Some were sadistic and took pleasure in our misery. They would mock us and make us talk to the wall. Sometimes, they would have us hold a leaf right in front of our eyes and stare at it cross-eyed while we talked to it. Or, they would pair us off and tell us to slap each other, forcing us to take turns hitting each other over and over again. Often, we would be told to sit down, spread our legs, and lean forward to touch our foreheads to the ground. While we strained to make it, the guards would jump on our backs, knocking the air from our lungs and wrenching our backs.

And always, always, there were the endless exercises. Sometimes more, sometimes less, varied in form and timing but always present.

Some inmates could not bear up under this kind of physical and mental strain. Quite a few of them went crazy and were sent to the mental institute. The pressure of prison life literally drove them out of their mind. Others turned suicidal. The lengths they would go in order to kill themselves were unbelievable. After one inmate hung himself, they cut our blankets down to a two-foot square; theorizing that it was impossible for someone to hang themselves with that. However, the truly desperate would always find a way to do themselves in.

As I endured the tortures, I struggled to be tough and tried to handle it. On the other hand, I was scared. There were prisoners in there with far worse characters than mine. I was always looking for a safe place or safe company. Everyone else was doing the same; just looking out for themselves. I didn't know a soul in there. Surely this was hell.

Gangs were a part of prison life. During my first few days, I was asked what group I was from. If I had been part of their group in the past, they would have let me in again. However, because I hadn't been part of a gang, I didn't seem to find my fit. Before long, I realized that you had to be with one group or another just for protection and to prevent yourself from going mad. Most inmates couldn't speak English, but since I could speak a bit, I joined with a few others who spoke English as well. This was our common ground and we formed a bond. Incredibly, I managed to stay neutral. You survive somehow.

8

TURPENTINE SMUGGLER

Later in my term, they implemented a work therapy program. We were allowed to go to work for a few hours a day in areas such as carpentry, farming, or laundry. We were paid fifteen cents a day, but the real reward was avoiding hours of exercise. I ended up working in the carpentry shop lacquering picture frames. There was an interesting side benefit: access to lacquer and turpentine. While working, we were constantly high from sniffing the fumes. People would go to any lengths to smuggle in this kind of substance, and here we were with it right under our noses.

Being so cramped together in our cell, some of the other inmates and I didn't get along. Living in a seven by ten-foot cell with someone you don't agree with is trouble. In those kinds of conditions, there were a hundred little ways to make each other's lives miserable if we wanted to. Finally, I saw a way to establish peace with everyone while indulging my own cravings in the comfort of my cell. I would smuggle in a can of turpentine for my cellmates. The task was far from simple. Every day when we came back to our cell we had to first go through a strip search at the main gate and then through a second gate where we were checked again. For days, I laid the groundwork, planned every detail, contacted the right people, made arrangements, and observed the guards. Finally, I was ready.

On one particular day, I brought two large, identical coffee mugs to the workshop. When the guards weren't watching, I half-filled the bottom mug with turpentine and fit the other mug inside.

That night, by the time I came to the main gate, I had already stripped down and had my clothes ready for inspection. As I approached the guard, right away he said, "OK, let's see what you have in there," gesturing towards the two containers. As I showed him the contents of the top container, I made a show of dropping my clothes on the floor. I bent over to pick them up, thus keeping the containers as far from him as possible. As I straightened up, apologizing, he just stood there with his hand still out waiting for the containers. I stood up and placed the bundle of clothes in his outstretched hand instead. He checked them over thoroughly, checking the seams, the waistband, and anywhere else that could conceal so much as a pin. Satisfied, he handed them back, and I draped them over my arm, covering the containers in the process. Out of sight, out of mind. He passed me through.

When I pulled that can out in my cell, I was instantly awarded hero status. The inmates were slapping me on the back with congratulations. What a ridiculous thing to be proud of, but I was. We discussed the turpentine and decided to wait until midnight to bring it out. By then, we could be sure that most of the guards would be asleep and there would be no surprise inspections. Of course, we chose a night when Sergeant Dan wouldn't be on duty, so there would be no chance of a blanket party to mess up our plan.

Finally, the lights went out, and everyone turned in to sleep: except for those in our cell. We lay awake in the dark waiting for midnight. In the silence, we could hear the slow pacing of the guard in the hall and the low snoring from the cells on either side. I lay back on the straw mat and stared at the moonlight cast high up on the wall. Time seemed to drag on and on.

It was time. Quietly, we crept to our hiding spot and removed the turpentine. Producing face cloths, we dipped them in the mug and held them to our nose. Soon we were high. The heady smell of turpentine filled the cell and seeped out under the door. Sniffing, the guard stopped in his rounds and pounded on our door. "Do you have turpentine in there?" he called in.

Feigning sleepiness, I called back, "No, sir, of course not. Please let us sleep." For a long moment, he waited at the door, and we held our breath.

If he unlocked the cell and came in, we were sure to be busted. With relief, we heard his footsteps receding down the hall, and we went back to our business.

The duty guard came back a couple of more times throughout the night, knocking on the door and questioning us, but we denied it all the way. Finally, just before we were supposed to get up, we tossed the turpentine-soaked cloths out the window. Down below, the first group of cooks knew to pick them up and get rid of them before anyone could see. We were able to discard all of the evidence except for the smell. That lingered thickly and filled every corner of our tiny cell. When the guards opened the door the next morning, they suspected what had happened immediately.

For some reason, they singled me out for interrogation. It just might have had something to do with the fact that I was the only one in my cell who worked in the carpentry shop. They took me to the interrogation room and were determined to find out the truth. With my hands chained overhead, all I could do was twist and groan while they kicked, punched, and slapped me.

As I slumped, hanging from the chains, the interrogating officer grabbed me by the jaw and raised my head, forcing me to look at him. His face was hard and tight with anger as he hissed, "You will tell us what you did last night, or we will make you wish you had never been born." Little did he know, I already wished I had never been born. I tried to shake my head, but he was holding my jaw too tight. Suddenly, he released me, smashing the back of his hand across my face. Pain slashed me, and I tasted blood. He turned his back and motioned to the others. "Carry on."

For the next few hours, I felt constant pain as the beating continued. Through it all, I was determined not to admit anything, knowing that a confession would only bring a harder beating and a longer sentence. Finally, they gave up trying to beat the truth out of me. They released me, and I collapsed to the floor, pain running up and down my body. I was sure I must have broken ribs. They dragged me back to my cell and dumped me inside. My cellmates fixed me up as best they could.

I was the hero of the hour to a bunch of decrepit, hopeless losers.

9

A FRIEND CALLED HONG

The next day, the cell door creaked open. Two guards came in and brought me to the commandant's office. He leaned back in his chair and toyed with a pen. "Xenn, I understand that you maintained your innocence in the turpentine episode that took place in your cell yesterday."

"Yes, sir," I replied calmly.

He made a show of examining the pen in his hand and then placed it carefully on his desk as he leaned forward. "I don't believe that for an instant. You're the only one in your cell with access to the carpentry shop." He stared at me for a long moment and then continued, "I've decided to let this go, but you are being relieved of your duties in carpentry. That is all." He motioned to the guards, "Take him back to his cell. Tomorrow, he starts back to regular exercises instead of work." Inwardly, I cringed as he fired that parting shot. Avoiding some of those brutal exercises was one of the main reasons I wanted to work in the first place.

That night, one of the guards, Hong, called me aside. During my time in that prison, I made two friends among the guards, and he was one of them.

He was around my age but slighter, shorter, and smaller than I was, with a pinched look to his narrow face. He had an easy going way about him that I liked. Why he was friendly with me, I don't know. Maybe he saw beyond what I could possibly see and felt that there was still some hope for me.

Smiling and cheery as usual, he said, "I heard what happened today, about you being taken out of the carpentry shop."

I was in no mood for his cheerfulness, especially concerning this subject, so I was shorter with him than usual when I replied, "So? You sure seem happy about it!"

Undaunted, he continued, still smiling, "I talked to the commandant and asked for you to be assigned to the farming section that I guard. He agreed!"

Instantly, my smile mirrored his. "Hong, you're a true friend. What can I say?"

He laughed, as he walked off. "Don't say anything. Just be ready to work tomorrow. I'm a real slave driver, you know!"

The next morning, Hong collected four other inmates and me who were assigned to the same farm detail. Off we went. The farm was small; just a few acres of field with a tiny, tin rest shack in one corner.

As we started into the field to work, Hong mused to himself loudly, "Well, I'm not really hungry for breakfast. I guess I'll just leave it here in the shack for now." Then he turned his back and walked to the far side of the field, looking out intently over the surroundings – everywhere but at us. We took the hint.

In a flash, we were digging into his bag and splitting the food among us. He'd brought some things with him that we never got in the prison, and this time we had more than five minutes to eat it. We ate slowly, savoring every bite and then went back to work with renewed vigor, determined that our new benefactor wouldn't get in trouble on our account. We did our best work for him. He never did mention his missing breakfast.

Our morning excursions to the farm became a daily ritual. We would walk to the field talking freely. We then ate breakfast and got to work. Hong was always pleasant. This was in sharp contrast with the other guards who were so often fierce and sadistic. Amid all the senseless brutality and torturous exercises, those mornings we spent together were times of refreshing. Hong's kindness was all the more compelling and magnetic because of the others' cruelty.

One day, he actually smuggled in a camera. A friendly tower guard took a picture of the two of us together with the other inmates and guard. Hong and I were standing side by side, smiling. With me in my frayed blue prison shorts and shaved head, and him in his crisp military police uniform, we made quite a pair.

Then one day, I found out that I was being transferred to another military prison, and I had to leave Hong and the farm. My heart was heavy. I wanted to cry, but of course, I was too tough for such nonsense. We drove for what seemed like a long time. At first, we traveled on paved roads then jolted off down dirt ones. We ventured deeper and deeper into the countryside: a place of fetid swamps and jungle growth. Finally, we pulled up in front of the prison gates, and I got my first glimpse of the living hell that would be my home for the next six months.

When the guards opened my cell door and pushed me inside, I immediately felt a vague uneasiness come over me. The tension in the air was palpable as the other inmates looked up from their huddle in the corner of the cell. The cell door closed behind me, and the lock chinked shut. I got the distinct feeling of being caged with a pack of lions. For a long time, they fixed me with dark stares that held no welcome, only anger and suspicion. They turned inward again, shutting me out as inconsequential.

I sank down in the opposite corner closer to the door. In the silence of the cell, the only sound was a constant scraping coming from their huddle. A couple of them were rocking back and forth, their shoulders working rhythmically.

Finally, when I couldn't bear the curiosity, I rose and crossed the couple of steps towards them to find out what they were doing. I only caught a glimpse of them rubbing toothbrushes on the floor before I felt the sharp point of one at my throat. In an instant, the inmate closest to me had sprung behind me, wrenched my arm into the small of my back, and pressed his weapon to my neck. The others rose slowly. Some had sharpened toothbrushes and some, double-edged razor blades slotted into toothbrush handles.

I knew I was looking at a gang just as surely as if they had been on the street brandishing knives and clubs. The one twisting my arm hissed into my ear, his foul breath washing over me, "Just keep your nose out of our business, and keep your mouth shut, you hear what I'm saying?" I could only nod carefully, the point still pricking my throat. Snarling, he said, "Good, now get back in your corner," as he spun me around and released his grip on my arm. I smashed against the wall and sank down. Suddenly, I just wasn't as curious anymore.

That night, I discovered one of the most miserable aspects of that prison. The low-lying swamp and sluggish, muddy rivers that surrounded the prison were an ideal breeding ground for the little beasts. At night, they came in swarms, settling on anything alive to feast and take their fill. I must have killed sixty of them that first night, yet I still woke up with itchy red bites all over my body. To this day, I have a deep, abiding loathing of mosquitoes that was birthed in that prison.

The next day, I discovered that between the brutality of the prisoners toward each other and the cruelty of the guards, this prison was worse than the last. As we were led to breakfast, two of my cellmates pounced on another prisoner; one stabbing him repeatedly in the neck with his sharpened toothbrush, the other slashing him with his razorblade imbedded toothbrush handle. Screaming, their victim fell to the ground as the guards charged in with batons flailing. The other prisoners observed the whole scene and then just continued to eat breakfast. I wasn't sure which was more unsettling: the scene of brutality or their calmness at viewing it. Obviously, this was not an uncommon occurrence for them.

After breakfast, we were taken out for exercises. If such a thing could be possible, the exercises were even more strenuous and torturous than those at the last prison. Seven man-made hills of hard packed earth and sand rose from the exercise grounds. The guards came down the line and strapped the familiar thirty-five-pound backpacks onto each prisoner's back. The ranking officer stood before us, reciting mechanically, "In single file, follow the path over the top of each hill. When you reach the end of the course, return by the same route. Right turn!" We each took a quarter turn to the right, leaving us in a long, single file line facing the beginning of the course. At his order, we started off one by one until the whole line was in motion.

At first, I was irritated at the pace set by those up ahead. They seemed painfully slow. However, I soon realized that the most experienced prisoners were pacing themselves for the long haul. We had seven hills to run up and down, twice. It was miserable. In some places, we struggled to advance where the path turned into sand, losing half the forward thrust of each step to the slipping surface underfoot. Reaching the crest of the first hill left me drenched in sweat.

With the weight on my back, maintaining my balance on the downhill slope was no easier. The backpack chaffed two spots just above the waistband of my shorts, gradually wearing the skin away. Each time my foot hit the ground, the backpack swung down onto those patches of raw flesh, bringing a fresh burst of agony. Finally, I was reduced to reaching back and holding up the pack as I ran.

Looking at the runners ahead of me, I could see that they also bore twin marks on their backs where the packs constantly rubbed. At the end of the day, the guards dashed iodine over the raw spots. Soon, I was to develop marks that never fully healed until after my release from prison. Even now, the bumpy, mottled scar tissue still remains, marking each of us that ran that race day after day for months on end.

One year passed, and finally, I was released. I left the constant cycle of fighting, gangs, exercises, and prison guards behind and returned directly to my army unit to continue the rest of my National Service.

When Hong heard that I was out of prison, he contacted me and we went out for coffee together. Sitting there in the coffeehouse, he gave me the picture of us together to remember him by. Somehow, after that, we drifted apart. Our lives were going in two different directions. His future lay in upholding the established system, and I was the poster boy for rebellion against that system.

I was too hardened to reform now. I had no choice but to return to my low life ways. Something in me was broken and could not be fixed. My future was already determined by my past. My dark hole of a life was dug far too deep to even dream of a better existence.

Because of the tough training and torturing in prison, I could safely say that the vast majority of everyone that was released relapsed back to drug addiction. The brutality of prison life, designed to break us of our habit, backfired. Instead, I had gone through so much that nothing could scare me anymore. I was tough and hardened to prison life through the duration of my sentences. The military's attempt to reform me ended in abject failure. How could they possibly think that such brutality could breed anything positive? The first day I was out, I was back on drugs.

10

INTELLIGENCE AND OPERATIONS

The klaxon shook me from sleep, blaring the wake-up call. With bleary eyes, I looked around me and forgot for a moment where I was. My surroundings were strange – a large room with bunk beds instead of my tiny cell. A moment later, I remembered. I'd been released from prison and sent back to my unit the day before. I fully expected to begin training and exercises with my unit again. Instead, I was summoned before the commanding officer.

Major Eric Young looked up from his desk as I entered the room. As I snapped to attention and saluted, he rose and returned my salute, motioning me to be seated. He flipped open the file folder centered on his desk and scanned its contents for a moment. I waited, wondering. Considering I had just been released from prison, I figured whatever he had to say about me and my record couldn't be good.

Finally, he looked up saying, "Xenn, it says here you are qualified to operate everything from basic small arms and bazookas to howitzers and armor. You're highly trained in intelligence operations and well versed in unit tactics. Is that correct?"

With the file open in front of him, my "Yes, sir. That is correct," was largely unnecessary.

He continued. "It seems you present me with a unique problem, private. You are simply over-qualified; too highly trained for simple duty as an average rifleman. Yet your past record excludes you from more sensitive positions."

I wasn't sure what to say at that point, so I just sat quietly. The conversation was definitely not what I expected.

"I've decided to post you to the intelligence and operations department as an assistant to the captain in charge. In spite of your past mistakes, I expect to hear good things about you in the future. You begin tomorrow. For today, enjoy yourself and acquaint yourself with the base here." He rose, and I rose with him. "That will be all."

Thanking him, I saluted and left, wondering at the change in my position and what effect it would have on the only thing I was really interested in – maintaining my drug habit.

He told me to enjoy myself and acquaint myself with the base, and I decided to take him up on it. Of course, he wouldn't have approved of my idea of enjoyment. Some of the previously released prisoners had already returned to the unit and had acquired drugs. I wasted no time in finding them and getting my first post-prison fix of marijuana. The appealing thing about marijuana was that I knew they couldn't test for it yet. After getting high, I set out to wander the base.

The base's original builders were obviously very British. Five, four-story buildings stretched their wings in towards the central parade square.

I wandered away from the square between the buildings until I ran up against the twelve-foot fence topped with barbwire that surrounded the compound. I followed it around the perimeter, passing open drill fields dotted here and there with platoons practicing maneuvers. I stopped for a while at the obstacle course and found a spot out of sight where I could overlook the proceedings. As I sat back, I laughed at the comical mishaps of those struggling under barbwire and over log walls, splashing into the mud with every slip and stumble. I was already beginning to enjoy being back. The smell of drugs and the taste of freedom made me heady.

Over time, I settled into a routine at the base, striking a balance between my duties and satisfying my drug habit. I managed to work myself into the good graces of my boss, the captain who ran the intelligence program. He allowed me a lot of freedom as long as I finished my work to his satisfaction. Of course, being an ex-convict, they made a point of restricting my access to any confidential material, but since I had already gone through so much training, I knew what they were talking about anyway. At this point, however, my only ambition was to stay high as much as possible.

Incredibly, my commanding officers seemed not to notice. More likely, they just chose to turn a blind eye to my more unorthodox behavior. Knowing that I was a favorite of the commanding officer, none of the sergeants or other officers questioned me as I made my way around the base. Many of them were afraid of me, while others respected my abilities. For one reason or another, the result was the same – they left me alone.

After a while, they trusted me enough to extend my duties to include being warden of the firing range. About twice a week there would be an outside booking for school cadets to use the firing range. Such bookings were done through me, and I was responsible for ordering targets and organizing their construction to meet the demand. I also taught the kids how to fire and clean their weapons. This turned out to be a highlight of my duties. I enjoyed interacting with normal, untainted people.

During this time, I developed a healthy respect for my commanding officer, Major Young. Under his command, our battalion was the best in the Singapore Infantry Regiment for three years running. Before long, he was given the rank of Colonel. One of the cornerstones of his successful training program was a series of extended unit maneuvers off the base.

On one such occasion, the whole battalion double-timed it across the parade ground in full gear, each platoon clambering swiftly aboard their assigned trucks. With the Major leading the column riding in his jeep and me following in the second jeep, we left for the training grounds in the open countryside.

When we reached our destination, the troops deployed with breathtaking precision, piling off the trucks, fanning out, clearing the area and rushing to secure their objectives. Throughout the day, it was like a constant, perfectly orchestrated dance, flowing effortlessly from strike to counterstrike. Through it all, the Major was the undisputed maestro. He stood in his command post plotting positions, radioing platoon leaders with their orders, and orchestrating the action of the far-flung battalion in harmonious, effective motion – a true master at work.

On the third night, he called me to his tent and announced that we were going out to inspect the platoons. Together with his driver, we drove to the first outpost. Rifle slung over my shoulder, I shadowed him as he approached and inspected the position; checking for proper entrenchment, clear lines of fire, and general condition of the troops. Afterward, he discussed the day's operation and that which was coming the next day with the platoon commanders. All the while, I kept a respectful distance. I heard their low, serious voices but did not intrude. I think I was just there for effect more than anything else. A full year of constant training and brutal exercise had increased my size and strength, making me an imposing figure. My presence lent the Major, who was a much smaller man, an extra aura of authority and sense of security.

When we finished our inspection, he turned to me with a mischievous twinkle in his eye and asked, "You wouldn't have any objection to swinging into town for a hot meal and then back to the base for a quick shower, would you?"

With a slight smile, I replied, "No, sir! You are in charge of this mission, sir!"

He smiled and said, "Mission indeed." He tapped the driver on the shoulder. "Our mission is to measure up to the standard set by the Military High Command. Please cooperate fully with their requests as they proceed with their inspection."

I heard the latter part of this announcement as I dashed in desperate fear of discovery, down the stairs and out the back door of the barracks. My heart was in my throat. All I could think about was the possibility of being pulled to the ground and handcuffed. Scenes from past prison sentences raced through my mind as I worked my way along the perimeter fence and behind the headquarters building. I sprinted into the inner hall, pounded up the stairs to the second floor, and almost fell through the major's doorway. The office was empty. I crouched, shaking behind his desk until the inspectors pulled out. This was my life in the army.

I enjoyed the respect I received from officers and soldiers alike due to my unique position as well as the larks I took with Major Young. All this while, I was overlooked by commanding officers that never seemed to notice the fact that I was constantly high. There were brief moments of near-discovery and terror, but in spite of these, I got comfortable and confident in the routine. Finally, my term in the army ended, and I was left to my own devices: a scary thought.

11

SURROUNDED AND CAPTURED

As an ex-convict, I was under supervision for two years after my release and was required to report to my probation officer regularly to submit a urine sample for testing. So I was always scheming, and constantly finding ways to dodge the tests and reports. Of course, in spite of all their efforts to protect me from myself, I managed to maintain my drug habit.

With my perception and reaction time lowered by the combination of drugs and alcohol flowing through my bloodstream, I raced down the road enjoying my freedom. Driving under the influence of drugs and alcohol became a very dangerous sport. It seemed that my four wheels were never on the ground at the same time. I was either careening down expressways, flying through the air, or skidding into ditches. Looking back, it amazes me that I didn't die in one of my many, many accidents. Any one of them certainly had the potential to do me in. Only much later did I realize that God had his hand on my senseless life.

Throughout this whole period, I didn't work in any one place for long. In spite of the fact that I never held a steady job, somehow I always had money. This fueled my rebellion against the structured life I led during my prison term and my time in the Service. I was making up for lost time. Inevitably, before long, it caught up with me. Again!

One day, I drove over to my friend's apartment to buy my daily ration of drugs. This was just a natural part of my routine.

The apartment was on the poor side of town. It was a dingy cement affair with tiny apartments stacked one on top of the other like human-sized cubbyholes. I passed the elevator. It was full of urine, bodily waste, and garbage, so I opted to climb the stairs instead. Garbage filled the landings as well. The smell was oppressive in the hot, unventilated air. After sprinting up the stairs to my friend's floor, I walked down the hall to his apartment. Only a dirty window at the far end of the hall cast light on the graffiti-painted walls and urine-puddled floor. Outside each apartment, bicycles and other odds and ends were piled haphazardly, narrowing the hallway until I could barely pass by. As a regular, I didn't even notice my dismal surroundings as I knocked on the solid wooden door.

My friend's little girl let me in. She was only six years old – a tiny little waif with deep eyes that always seemed sad and reproachful. It was as if she knew that she had a poor lot in life. She stepped aside quietly, as my friend called a welcome from his spot at the kitchen table. He was busy working with a scale and small packages of heroin.

The room was small and miserable. Two other customers, also friends of mine, were there as well. They were lounging on the threadbare couch and smoking up. Usually, I would just buy my drugs and leave. Today was different. Perhaps because two of my friends were there, or maybe because I just had nowhere else to go, I decided to stay on. I spent the next half-hour hanging out and smoking drugs with my friends.

Just as I had used up my fresh purchase of drugs, there was a knock on the door. My friend was obviously expecting a buyer who had pre-ordered because he called his daughter over and gave her a package to hand out at the door. Meanwhile, I walked to the open window hoping to catch a stray breeze wafting in. The constant heat and humidity in the room were almost unbearable. Movement from below caught my eye. Looking down, I swore, spinning away from the window. The little girl was at the door, throwing back the double bolts.

I shouted, "Don't open it, it's the narcs!" My warning came a moment too late. As the second bolt shot open, a narcotics officer put his shoulder to the door, slammed it open, and knocked the girl back against the wall.

They swarmed in with guns at the ready, shouting, "Get on the ground, get on the ground, now! Move it! Let me see your hands!"

I was forced to the ground, arms twisted up behind my back, and handcuffed. The voice of my friend's little girl sadly carried over the shouts and commotion. She was crying. Irrationally, I blamed the police for that. Then they dragged us away.

Because I had already finished the drugs I had bought that day, they couldn't charge me with possession or drug use right away. Instead, they locked me away, took my urine sample for analysis, and observed me, looking for withdrawal symptoms. Cut off drugs cold turkey like that, the withdrawals were not long in coming. I could eat, but I couldn't keep it down, and I had constant diarrhea. My stomach cramped horribly.

I lay curled into a ball on the floor of my room for as long as I could stand it before crawling painfully down to the washroom. Dragging myself into the shower, I reached up, fumbled for the handles, and turned the cold water on full blast. To anyone going through withdrawals, the slightest hint of cold is unbearable. Even the air movement from a fan is torturous. Yet, I knelt there on the cement floor of the shower stall with cold water beating down on me. It was the only way to make the withdrawal symptoms subside. After ten minutes, I reached up and shut off the water. I shook with a chill as I climbed out of the shower and began toweling myself off. By the time I was dry, the symptoms had almost completely subsided, and I could walk down the hall to my room.

No sooner had I laid down, however, the symptoms returned with a fury, and the vicious cycle started all over again. This period of intense withdrawals continued for the first week before easing off. Once again, after the physical withdrawals, came the psychological withdrawals. The whole process took about two months.

Of course, by then it was obvious to anyone watching that I had been using drugs. Considering the duration of my withdrawal symptoms, it was clear that I was not just a user – I was an addict. Their observations held more than sufficient evidence to convict me, and by this time they also had the evidence from my urine sample. I found myself behind bars once more but this time serving an eighteen-month sentence without parole.

Instead of a cell, I was placed in a dormitory. It was crowded with a hundred and twenty inmates in a space of fifty by fifty feet – Indians, Chinese, and Malays were all mixed together. Long fluorescent light bulbs in fine mesh metal grills cast industrial type lighting over the room. Sixty bunk beds lined the central aisle.

At the time, Singapore had five such facilities which they called Drug Rehabilitation Centers (DRCs). Unlike those in the US where you voluntarily checked yourself in, these DRCs were, in fact, prisons. Locked cells, security guards, strict discipline, and brutal punishments were the norm. Singapore even had glue sniffing penalties and lock-ups.

Many prisoners not only had drug dependency problems but also other criminal cases pending for crimes they committed to support their drug habit. Some were in for two to four years for drugs alone, and then they would face these court cases and further sentences upon their release. For far too many, this endless cycle of drugs, crime, and prison becomes a lifestyle.

Because most drug addicts in Singapore cut their teeth on heroin and morphine instead of marijuana, addiction comes fast and hard. Teens become junkies easier and faster, and many have family problems due to years of hurting their loved ones while taking drugs. I was no exception. However, even though my family was embarrassed, hurt, and disappointed by me, they still stood by me. Even though I could see the pain I caused them, they never turned their back on me. I may not have realized it at the time, but they were my only stability in life.

Drug addicts live in a subculture far below the radar of a social culture which they can't seem to function in very well. Within that subculture, they have their own laws, rules, and way of life. Just as they can't seem to survive in a social culture, most people would never survive in their subculture. I was a part of that subculture, and I couldn't escape. I couldn't change. I was caught up in an endless, hopeless cycle.

After a few months, I was put to work in the income scheme office where I kept track of the money earned by the four hundred prisoners in their work therapy programs. They were able to use this money every weekend to purchase little luxuries from the canteen. I was in charge of ordering some of the rations for this canteen.

In the process, I realized that one of the officers in charge was buying expired and sub-standard products for the canteen at lower prices and pocketing the balance. Unwisely, I approached him about it, and we argued fiercely. Finally, he went to the prison authorities and somehow convinced them that I was dangerous and should be transferred out of the prison. And so, I found myself bouncing and jostling in the back of the prison van toward a maximum security prison to take my place among criminals, kidnappers, and murderers.

12

MAXIMUM SECURITY PRISON

The prison van made a final turn and came to a stop at a set of huge steel gates. The gates opened to admit us. We drove through and stopped again as these gates clanged shut behind us. Looking out through the small back window, the twenty-five-foot wall, topped with barbwire, stretched off in either direction as far as I could see. The second set of gates opened, and we drove into the prison yard. Behind me, I could hear dogs barking as a patrol car drove by. Guards paced back and forth in the towers commanding the walls. The M16s they held weren't just for looks. I learned later that the guards were from Nepal. They were crack shots – trained to shoot to kill. No one ever escaped from Singapore's Changi prison.

The British originally built the prison. It served as a POW camp during the Japanese occupation in the Second World War. It was a huge prison with six cell blocks, each five stories high. The blocks were built like apartment buildings, but instead of apartments, there were tiny cells holding three or four prisoners each. This prison was one huge pool of human misery, and I was right in the middle of it all.

I had learned from my experience at the last prison not to be too forward when I was assigned to my cell. I just entered quietly, found my empty space on the floor, then spread out my floor mat and blanket. I lay down and kept to myself, deciding to let my three cellmates approach me if they were so inclined. Until then, I would just give them time to look me over and get used to me. Meanwhile, I looked around the room. It was small, measuring maybe seven by ten feet. We all had straw mats and blankets for sleeping but no pillows. The only other feature was the toilet in the corner. At least we had that luxury, I thought.

The next morning, I suddenly awoke to shrill screaming. I sat up and searched with my ears to try and place the awful sound. One of the other inmates looked over and smiled grimly, saying, "Ah, you've never heard the execution symphony before. Don't worry, you'll get used to it. We're close to the condemned cells, and it happens every month. Listen, hear the screams? It's 6 a.m. on the button. They've come to bring him out of his cell, and he's so scared he can't even move. All he can do is scream. Now they'll be dragging him out into the gallows chamber, and he's messing his drawers. Of course, some of them don't react. Some are tougher than that, but most break down – like him. He knows he's in his last hour. Now they'll be leading him out to the scaffold. Probably have to carry him most of the way. They'll be holding him up while they put the rope around his neck so he won't slump over and start the show early. And now, if you listen real close, you can hear the clunk as they throw the lever and the trap door falls open and bangs against the scaffold. You can only hear him hit the end of the rope if it's really, really quiet."

My throat tightened up and then landed in the pit of my stomach. I became aware of the fact that I was staring at him. He seemed to take such a deep, morbid interest in the executions. I wondered what this brute was in there for - not that I dared to ask him.

Then he smiled, showing broken yellowed teeth. "My name is Xinghao. Who are you?" he asked.

It seemed I had made a friend. I introduced myself, and he dragged me over to meet the other two cellmates. We spent the morning sitting around talking and getting to know about each other and our sordid pasts.

At 8 a.m., we were interrupted by a guard who knocked on the door and brought us our breakfast. It was nothing great, as usual, just two slices of bread and some weak coffee. The guard slid the food in through the slot in the door and then latched the flap shut again. I was just stuffing the last bit of bread in my mouth when Xinghao turned to me and asked, "So! Know any stories?"

Surprised at the sudden conversation curveball, I asked, "Stories? Ya sure, but that's a funny question isn't it?"

He laughed ruefully, and added, "I guess so, but we've been in here so long that we've told each other all the stories we know. Now we've run out, so we were hoping you'd have some new ones."

So I started to tell stories. I told them about my first break-in, and they laughed at how we went to all that trouble just to steal a goldfish. Then I told them about one of the gang crashes I'd seen, and that got them started too. I guess having someone new to tell their old stories to made it worth telling them again. Lying around the cell, we swapped stories throughout the day. There was simply nothing else to do. We spent twenty-three and a half hours locked away in our cell with a half-hour shower break.

At lunchtime, the guard followed the same procedure of knocking on the door and sliding in the trays of food. This time, the selection was a bit better: tofu, rice, soup, and some vegetables. My new friends saw me eyeing the cubes of tofu suspiciously and laughed. According to them, we would get this stuff every day, and I would soon get used to it. Every once in a while, we got pork or fish, and chicken was on the menu once a month. The tofu was soggy inside and almost tasteless, but they were right. With nothing else to eat, I adapted to it over time.

So we told more stories – stories about ourselves and other people that we had heard about. Often we exaggerated to make the characters more heroic than they really were. After so many days, we ran out of stories to tell. So, we made them up and passed them off as real. If the others had realized this, they never seemed to mind. It was still entertainment, but even our imagination had limits. The overwhelming feeling of being in that prison was that of boredom.

After a while, we had absolutely nothing to do. Nothing to read, nothing to see, nothing to talk about. Nothing! We began to think of the trouble we could get into and planned what mischief we could stir up.

As the end of the month came closer, we started to get excited. Month's end meant family visits and the little treats they were allowed to bring us. Finally, the day came, and it was pandemonium. The visitors' area was jam packed with inmates and family members, their hands waving wildly to get each other's attention. Somehow, I fought my way to where my mother was calling my name. She had brought me two kilograms of biscuits and peanuts. All too soon, she had to leave. Even though I looked forward to her visit, I dreaded to see the pain in her eyes. I knew her heart ached for her only son, but there was very little I could do.

Back in the cell, my friends were all business. We pooled our peanuts and counted them out carefully on a blanket. Xinghao sat back and rubbed his hands together contentedly, "Ah yes, many tobaccos, many tobaccos with these."

We had already made arrangements with the "Section 55" prisoners. They were imprisoned without trial and lived two floors below us. Their families were allowed to bring them tobacco, and they'd agreed to sell us some in exchange for peanuts.

That night, instead of going to sleep as usual, our cell was a flurry of activity. Carefully, we pulled several long strings from our blankets and tied them together. To one end, we attached a toothbrush. Meanwhile, one of my cellmates was making rolls out of magazine pages we had smuggled in for our purpose. We poured the peanuts into these and then folded in the ends, twisting them securely shut.

While all these preparations were being made, another inmate called down the toilet pipe to the floor below us, "Cargo coming down!"

Below, we heard the inmates relay the message down in like manner, "Cargo coming down!"

Xinghao stood on my shoulders, feeding the toothbrush and string out through the window. The bars formed a crosshatch pattern with only one-inch openings between them. Over each window was a two-foot cement awning to keep the rain out. As we lowered the toothbrush on the string, the awning held it two feet out from their window. Originally, this had caused a bit of a problem, but with so much time on their hands, the inmates had soon figured out a solution. They launched out a toothbrush and string of their own to loop around ours to drag it in. The message returned, echoing up through the pipe, "Ready, send it down!" We fed out the peanut rolls in a long line like a string of uncut sausages.

On a moonlit night, an observer from outside could have seen scores of these paper rolls running up and down the sides of the cellblock.

When the last one was down, they called again, "Cargo coming up!" and we reeled in our string, this time with tobacco loaded rolls instead of the peanuts. One roll also held a bit of flint stone. Striking the flint stone with a bit of fluff from our blankets, we managed to start a fire to light our cigarettes. We leaned back and exhaled clouds of smoke with satisfied sighs.

Suddenly, Xinghao swore and started searching through the paper rolls. Finally, he came up with a tiny block of ink. He held it up smiling and said, "Time for a new tattoo!" Then he slapped his head. "Stupid! I still have to pay! Here, give me a hand," he said.

Rerolling part of his tobacco, he tied it to a long piece of string and went over to the door. In a low voice, he called down the hall, "Cargo coming over for room eight!"

Room eight was three doors down. This was a problem. The cell doors were paired up in twos, side by side, and then a long section of wall before the next two doors. Somehow, we had to pass it three doors down and across two long sections of wall.

With a practiced hand, Xinghao rolled the tobacco out into the hall and through a spot under the door, while holding onto the string. The roll arched toward the next cell and slid under their door. They then passed it to the cell next to them. This technique was repeated until the roll reached its final destination. I never saw a man so determined to make his payments before.

Then came the challenging part. Somehow, Xinghao had to get himself into the tattooing cell down the hall. He made the switch during our half-hour shower break. They ushered us, one cell at a time, to the shower stalls. As our cell was on the way back, another cell was opened for the same routine. One of the second group of inmates switched places with Xinghao, and off he went back to the showers again. This process was continued until he got two doors down to the makeshift tattooing parlor. By the time he got there, he was definitely clean. The next day, once the tattoo was finished, he would use the same means to get back to our cell.

Sometimes, we used this method for more violent means, like settling a score with someone from the other side of the cellblock. We went to elaborate extents to conduct our business. Such attacks and cell switching bore a stiff penalty, but it was a risk we were willing to take.

After seven months of this endless cycle of boredom, punctuated with brief moments of forbidden thrills and sudden danger, they sent me to a Day Release Program. According to this program, prisoners went to work for local companies during the day and came back to the prison at night. I'm not sure by what merit, but I was selected for this privilege.

A very good friend of mine agreed to take me under his charge. In theory, he applied for me to work at the real estate agency that he owned, but he didn't expect me to do any work. He allowed me the freedom to do whatever I wanted and even supplied me with a car. Of course, I used it to get to and from my drug supplier as well.

Even though we were good buddies, I never saw my friend after I was released. It was probably due to the fact that he used to be a drug user in the past but had quit his habit. For his own sake, he made the right decision to stay as far away from me as possible.

After six months of this program, I was finally released on two years of supervision. Once again, I had to routinely report to my officer and give my urine sample to make sure I wasn't back on heroin again. This substance was detectable in urine samples. In spite of all their efforts, however, I continued to use drugs. I was now getting into heavier and heavier transactions and consuming more and more drugs. All their efforts to reform me failed, and I was hitting rock bottom fast. Ultimately, I did change while in prison but in a most unexpected way.

13

"JESUS, HELP ME!"

Many of the men I spent time in prison with amazed me with their talents and capabilities, yet they had begun drug use in their early teens and could never escape the diabolical web it wove. Most didn't really have the heart to change. They were just serving time because they were caught. As any drug addict or alcoholic knows, you need a complete change of mind, will, and heart, or you will immediately end up right back at square one the moment you are released.

Like most addicts, my time in prison did not reform me in the least. Left to my own devices, I was bound to fail when pressure came my way. Many can do well for a few years, but when disappointments, hurts, or failures come knocking, they resort back to the same old patterns of coping. I had never learned any other way. Careful nurturing with positive examples and direction was not a part of my upbringing. My answer to adversity was to get wasted.

For the next seven years, I did very well and managed to escape arrest. All the while, I was enjoying a life of drinking and club hopping. I avoided arrest because, by now, I'd learned from my mistakes. Instead of maintaining my previous routine of buying drugs daily, I now bought my drugs less often. Without having to get it every day, my chances of arrest were minimized.

And so, it happened one Sunday in 1990. Early in the month, I knocked on yet another solid wooden door, in the shadows of yet another filthy hallway, in yet another run-down tenement. This time, I didn't hang around. After checking me out through the peephole, the supplier handed out the white powder. I handed in the money, tucked the package inside my shirt, and was gone.

That night, as usual, I was high. The next morning, I was still snoring when there was a sound outside at my door. There was a short grunt of effort and then a sharp snap as the padlock on my metal gate was cut. Still, I slept. Next came a wrenching sound of a crowbar twisting metal as my door started taking punishment. The door was solid and was fastened with a Chubb deadbolt like banks use. Not easy to breach! The struggle to enter my apartment went on for almost an hour, yet I never woke up. Of course, most addicts sleep until the afternoon, so that was hardly surprising.

The sounds of ransacking and searching came from my kitchen, storage room, and the rest of the apartment. Tables flipping over, couch cushions being ripped open, books and papers spilling to the floor.

Finally, the noise woke me up, but I lay there still groggy from sleep. Looking at the gap at the bottom of my bedroom door, I could see shadows moving up and down the floor outside. My first thought was that my mother was home, so I got up and opened the door. It was a mistake!

There were law enforcers in my apartment. My eyes flew wide open, and I slammed the door closed. I didn't stand a chance as I fumbled to relock it. The four narcotics officers slammed their shoulders against the door on the other side, and I was knocked backward. They rushed in and threw me to the floor.

The next thing I knew, I was sitting on the bed with my hands cuffed behind my back. I was now a desperate man. If they were to find out what I had in my room, I would be in more than just big trouble.

In that instant, knowing I was surely caught, I cried out, "Jesus, help me! Jesus, help me!" The words just rolled out of my mouth. That dying feeling was all over me, and I thought, "That's it, I need help." It was obvious to me that I needed something or someone bigger than I to help me out of this mess.

The first words that the officer said were, "Bring out the drugs. Tell us where you keep them."

I just shook my head and denied it. "I don't have any with me," I said.

The back of his hand smacked hard against my cheek, and I tasted blood. He demanded again, "I know you have them in here, and you know that we'll find them. The only thing you can control is how much punishment you take before we do. Now tell us!"

While he questioned me, the other three officers began methodically ransacking my room as they tried to locate the drugs. In a few seconds, the place was destroyed.

I refused to admit anything as I sat there in silence. Incensed, he started punching and kicking me. I felt pain crash through my skull and a sick feeling flow in to fill my stomach. For a moment, he paused, visibly struggling to control himself. He then leaned in close and hissed, "Listen to me, right here, right now. Do you want to know why I'm so sure you have the drugs in here? Because an informant passed me the information! He fingered you." As if re-enacting it, he jabbed me in the chest with a hard forefinger. "You! Now you're going down, one way or the other. Easy ... or hard!" He grunted out the last word as his fist smashed into my jaw; punctuating his statement with an exclamation point of pain.

My heart stopped, as I cast a sidelong glance at the other officers. One was poised just in front of my bedside table. He wrenched open the drawer and started sifting through the junk and jumble inside. All the evidence he would have needed was sitting there right in front of his eyes. From three or four feet away, I could see the drugs mixing around in the drawer as he fingered through them. Incredibly, he couldn't see the packages. Finally, he slammed the drawer shut, and I drew a deep breath. I was unaware that I'd been holding my breath. All the while, I had carefully averted my eyes to other parts of the room to keep from giving away the location of the drugs.

As their whirlwind search failed to turn up any evidence, they continued to beat me up. A fist crashed into my ribs, driving all air from my lungs. And then the next moment, I found I couldn't breathe anyway because another officer had yanked open the same drawer again and was again rooting through it. Unbelievably, he didn't see the drugs either. Meanwhile, the other officers were overturning the mattress, checking my closet, digging through my shirts, and searching every square inch of my room. Not one of them realized that the drugs were right there under their noses. I know now, that Jesus blinded their eyes. Not because He approved of my sin but because He loved me, died for me, and still had a plan for me.

I was on a knife's edge, a second away from discovery.

The Singapore law is so strict that, in some situations, the penalty for drug use can even mean death by hanging.

Finally, I looked the conducting officer straight in the eye and said, "sir, please don't beat me if you can't find anything in my apartment."

For a long time, he looked hard into my eyes, obviously trying to tell whether he could believe me or not. Finally, he made the decision and told the other officers, "Let's go, we'll take him to the station."

Handcuffed, they propelled me down the hall, into an unmarked police cruiser, and into the station. As per standard practice, they took my urine sample and my statement. Knowing that my urine tests would undoubtedly come back positive, I admitted that I consumed but maintained that I didn't have any drugs with me.

All the while, I was trying to cooperate with them so that I could make a phone call to my mom. I politely asked the officer, "Could I please make a phone call to my mom?"

"No," he replied curtly.

I pleaded with him, finally querying, "Would you want to be responsible if any of my property went missing from my apartment?"

Relenting, he agreed to let me make one quick phone call, but he stood next to me all the while. I dialed my mom and she picked up the phone. I said, "Mom, I'm at the police station."

Her first words were, "Are you going to die?"

"No," I said flatly.

She asked, "Do you still have anything in your apartment?"

"Yes," I said.

With the inspector standing right there, yes and no answers were all I could dare. But I had to take a chance, so I continued, "Can you please go and take care of my apartment? Everything is all messed up, and the table is upside down."

She caught the hint and shot back right away, "Do you mean you have it in the table in your bedroom?"

With a final, "Yes," I put down the phone.

What I had been hiding to protect her, she now destroyed to protect me. My mom took the initiative to flush the drugs down the toilet. Her last words on the phone rang in my ears as I hung up. "Only Jesus can help you now," she said. Where did that come from? My mother was not a Christian but a Buddhist. Why was she talking about Jesus?

14

"I WANT TO CHANGE"

After giving my statement and calling my mother, they sent me into the holding cell for the night. The lock-up cell was especially terrible this time. The filth and stench of ten unwashed bodies crammed into one little room made it almost unbearable. Sitting there against the wall, I shivered and yawned. I just didn't want to move, even if I could. I felt completely drained. My joints screamed in protest when I tried to straighten out my legs, and my cramped stomach made me draw my knees back up to my chest. I knew the symptoms all too well; already, I was going into withdrawals. Soon, the heavy withdrawals would come, and I sat there trying to fight them off. They came anyway, and there was nothing I could do about it. With that certain knowledge, I spent the night in misery.

The next day, I was sent back to prison for a week of cold turkey under observation. The physical and psychological withdrawals started again: cramps, diarrhea, weakness, ultra-sensitivity to cold. I suffered through the same old cycle, doubled over in my cell. I crawled to a cold shower and walked back to my cell feeling a bit better, only to double over in pain again as soon as I got back. This time around was much worse than the last. It was almost three months before my body felt normal again.

When the doors slammed shut behind me, I switched to my prison mindset. It was like throwing a mental switch off and on. It was my coping mechanism – my only way to keep from going crazy.

After the withdrawals were over, I was transferred to a dormitory. There were twenty-four of us in a room about thirty-five by fifteen feet. This was barely enough room to lie down. I was so weary in mind and body, and I wondered if I could survive this one more time.

The next morning, the guards came to take us to the yard. I was shocked to realize that getting outside was now part of our routine. We didn't have to beg and plead to get some fresh air. Obviously, the program had changed. Now, they let us out for a short time every weekday. We were even allowed to take as many showers as we wanted! This place seemed like a hotel compared to the last.

During this stay, I was put in charge of the kitchen. My responsibilities were to order the food and make sure it was prepared to expectations. Unfortunately, my responsibility also extended over the kitchen staff, a good number of whom stayed in my dormitory. If fights broke out, as they often did, the guards would pull me aside and demand information on what happened and who was involved. This put me in an awkward spot, and so the best policy was to always plead ignorance.

I knew that even without my testimony they would investigate and get to the bottom of these situations. Then they would press charges of assault and fighting that could extend a prisoner's sentence. I knew better than to get involved. It was my head if I did.

A lot more was going on in the kitchen besides preparing food. We were also a delivery service of sorts. We slipped little packages of goodies into certain marked containers of food and then covered them carefully with mounds of rice. Special foodstuffs went into some. Others got needles or ink for tattooing, still others received tobacco. We smuggled for friends regularly.

After several months, my responsible conduct in running the kitchen brought me before the superintendent of the prison. As I entered his office, he rose and smiled, motioning me to a chair. We sat down.

He started, "I've noticed the work you've been doing in the kitchen. You've done a good job there."

"Thank you, sir."

"In all your months here, you have stayed out of trouble and avoided fighting, is that true?"

"Yes, sir."

He leaned back in his chair. "Why is that?"

"Well, I suppose because I haven't had anything to fight about, sir."

He smiled, "That never seems to stop the other prisoners. Xenn, I like you. I think you have the makings of a good man. I've recommended you for early release. In the meanwhile, you're being transferred to a new prison where you'll be allowed out on a day pass to work for the rest of your sentence. I think you're ready to start going back outside. I have faith in you."

As it turned out, his faith in me was not justified. The next day, I pulled up to my new job, walked into the boss' office, and gave her a big hug – she was my sister. She let me know that she wasn't going to make heavy demands on me in her company. She just wanted to see me out. I felt so grateful to her. I had given her nothing but heartache, and here she was trying to make my life a little more comfortable.

I had the freedom to go anywhere and do anything I wanted. This was not a good thing. I spent my days hanging out with friends and getting into the same old trouble as before. I went back to the prison every evening for a good night's sleep. The rest of my prison term was spent like this. It was a pretty easy life, but I was still looking forward to total freedom.

The day of my release drew closer and closer. Finally, I walked down the hall to collect my ID card. I was itching to get out of there. Freedom was so close I could taste it.

And then it happened. As luck would have it, they were doing spot checks and pulled me from the line for a urine test. I knew I was finished. Of course, the test came back positive, and they locked me up again. I'd gone back to drug abuse. The superintendent, his trust in me betrayed, was determined to keep me for a long time. All my previous privileges were reversed, and I spent my days in boredom, confined to my dormitory. Depression wrapped itself around me.

This was when my life began to miraculously change. The prison had a few programs here and there to cut the boredom. One of these programs was a chapel service. When the prison clerk came to invite me to attend, I was primed to go. I had absolutely nothing else to do, and so I went willingly.

When I opened the door to the chapel, there was a group of people singing songs about Jesus. The music washed over me as I found a place to sit down. By the time I was seated, tears were rolling down my face. Angry and confused, I brushed them away. This was unacceptable. This was prison, and the only code of conduct was to be tough. I knew that if the other guys saw my tears, I would be mocked.

The American lady at the front of the room seemed to have a glow about her. She looked kind, and I saw that she was filled with joy as she sang. These songs seemed to have a strange effect on her. When I saw Genny Miller for the first time, I couldn't know that she was to play such an important role in my life. In time, she was to become a very special friend and mentor.

I didn't know why I had cried that first week, but when I arrived at the service again the next week, I was determined to keep a straight face. I steeled myself outside the door before walking in. "Don't cry, don't cry, don't cry," I told myself. Yet again, the tears streamed down my face. It seemed to make no sense to me. Never before, not even when I was under torture, had I cried as much as I did now. When I left, I was frustrated at my own weakness and lack of control. Something drew me back, though. I felt compelled to attend those services.

Many of the boys who attended the chapel services were not the least bit interested in God, worship, or real change. Instead, they saw this as a great time to play. It was a good place to pass information and plan their shifty schemes. There were always a lot of clowns in the bunch. By the third week, I joined in the fun and games and was determined to make as much mischief in the service as possible. I talked loudly to the inmates beside me, laughing and joking all the way. Still, they went on with the service, singing and talking about this Jesus that I knew nothing about. Before long, the tears ran down my face again. Finally, I had to admit to myself that there was something different in this place.

All the while, I had tried to appear tough on the outside, but on the inside, God was tenderizing me. Upon hearing the Gospel, my inner man started to cry out and respond in a way my tough exterior couldn't hide. Almost against my will, my spiritual hunger forced me to press forward and grab hold of something real from God in order to survive.

When I went back to my dormitory that night, I couldn't sleep. This American lady talked about prayer. I didn't know the first thing about this, but I wanted to give it a try. I waited up until all of my cellmates had fallen asleep and then I began to talk. I felt foolish. Who was I talking to? I felt like I was talking to the air.

I'd been to three Bible studies already, but I still didn't know the first thing about God. So I simply said, "Jesus, I want to change. Please help me to change." I kind of made a bargain with God. I said, "God let me out of here. I don't want this life anymore. If you let me out of here in six months, I will serve you." In my innocent mind, this was how I knew to pray.

I didn't know it yet, but I lived in a second prison, one that was even more brutal and restrictive than the DRCs in Singapore. I was in bondage to Satan and his vices. Now for the first time, after being locked away for years in torment and darkness, a beam of light pierced the walls and bars. Love and light began to penetrate my heart, and although I didn't understand it all, I wanted to know more. As Jesus said in John 8:12, *"...I am the light of the world: he that followeth me shall not walk in darkness, but shall have the light of life."* Before long, His love would break my chains, and I would follow Him out of the darkness of my spiritual prison, into the glory of His marvelous light.

At about three in the morning, a friendly prison guard came on duty and asked me why I was still up. I simply told him that I couldn't sleep. He just said, "Well, don't stay up too late." Taking his advice, I let myself fall asleep. In the months to come, that prayer slipped from my mind. But somewhere beyond those walls, the One who hears all prayers bent his ear to a Singapore cell and heard a miserable prisoner's simple words. He had a plan for me.

15

ROTAN CANING

II Chronicles 16:9 states, *"For the eyes of the LORD run to and fro throughout the whole earth, to shew himself strong in the behalf of them whose heart is perfect toward him..."* That pretty much describes my spiritual life in prison for the remainder of my term. The Lord was strengthening me as I was seeking after Him, trying to learn more about this God who cared enough to die for me.

I was far from a saint, but slowly a change was coming over me. I continued to go to the chapel services faithfully, and I started to read the Bible. I no longer mixed around with the rough crowd, and I isolated myself from the tattooing, smuggling, and fighting. Yet, with this new beginning, there were many conflicts with the other inmates when I decided not to cooperate with them. Teamwork was needed to pull off the many illegal dealings we got mixed up within the prison. Anyone who didn't get involved was suspect. Only in the chapel services did I feel truly safe. Life continued with a kind of nervous, edgy rhythm.

One day, the order came down for me to receive a most brutal punishment: a *rotan* caning. I was considered a hard-core addict by now, and this was my due reward. On that fateful morning, the cell door swung open and the guards ushered me out. We hopped into a waiting van for a quick ride to the yard where I would be subjected to three strokes.

All the way there, my mind was whirling. Caning was a common punishment for addicts and pushers, so there had been lots of talk about what to expect. I had heard it was one of the most painful means of reform. This particular outing was not going to be a picnic.

The guards led me towards a wooden holding stage in the prison yard and tied me down. The brawny warder stood to one side with the seven foot *rotan* cane. By now, I was resigned to my fate. I was stripped naked, as my hands were tied together and my feet tied apart. Then I was bent over the wooden frame with a broad leather pad belted around my waist. At least they were merciful enough to only want to make contact with a fleshy bottom. As one of the guards secured my hands, he said, in a voice strangely calm and gentle, "It's OK. Just take your caning, go home, and sleep. It'll all be over in a minute."

Maybe he was right about the time, but to me, tied there vulnerable and bare, it seemed like an eternity. Behind me, I could hear the *"voop voop voop"* as the warder swung the cane in circles over his head. He was just warming up. Every second of the wait was agony.

The warder ran up behind me with three fast, thudding steps. In that split second, I heard the zip of the cane as it arced downwards.

PAIN! Pain writhed all over my body. It spread everywhere. By the time I could take a good breath, the second stroke exploded across my backside. I never even felt the third stroke; by that time, I was just numb. When they released me, my legs wobbled and I almost fell. A doctor was there to examine me. He splashed some iodine across the three bloody, parallel slashes, and that was it. I was sent back to the van for transport back to the prison.

As we jounced along the road, I could not sit down for the ride. With blood soaking into my shorts, I spent the whole trip holding myself up off the seat with my hands. I wasn't even offered a painkiller.

Back at the dormitory, I immediately went for a shower. Soaking my shorts with water, I loosened the dried blood to avoid disturbing the wounds. I washed the raw, open wounds with soap, wincing at the sharp sting and then dressed them as best I could with toilet paper. Once I reached my dorm, I paced up and down. I couldn't even sit. We had chapel service that very afternoon, and I decided to attend anyway, regardless of my insulting morning.

Besides Genny Miller, Rev. Steve Willoughby, Missionary to Singapore, also conducted Bible studies during the chapel service. He gave me a strange look when I resisted his order for everyone to sit down. Thankfully, he let it go. He didn't know that I had been caned until the day I was released when he asked me about the incident. With a straightforward stare, I replied, "Actually, I was caned that morning."

He was in shock, "And you still came! You seemed so calm, so natural!" He couldn't believe his ears. Most prisoners who have been caned, spend the next few days lying on their face in their cell waiting for their wounds to start healing. I just felt that I needed to be in that service.

I attended the chapel service every week without fail, and Jesus began to become more and more real to me. Slowly, He began to bind my inner wounds and open up my spiritual awareness and understanding. I was amazed.

These people were also beginning to work their way into my heart, and they were quickly becoming my friends. In fact, that year I decided not to celebrate Chinese New Year, but instead, I celebrated Christmas with them. I had always celebrated Chinese New Year; it was my tradition. However, now it just didn't seem very important in comparison. It was prison policy that we were only able to celebrate one holiday or the other. The choice was an easy one to make.

The days were slowly ticking by, and then it happened. Five months and twenty-nine days after my prayer for release, at 5 p.m. in the evening, an officer came and escorted me to the superintendent's office. This was the same superintendent that had first recommended me for early release and then determined to keep me incarcerated for as long as possible. When I walked in, he turned from the window to face me; his face grim, his mouth turned down at the corners, his eyes cold. He looked at me and struggled to keep his voice level as he said, "Tomorrow you are being released."

I looked at him and kind of smiled. I said, "Sir, you must be joking." I was stalling, buying time, trying to figure it out. My mind was racing. I thought that maybe he wanted to exchange information for freedom. Maybe someone had escaped, or maybe some sort of shifty business had been discovered in the prison.

Staring me straight in the eyes, he repeated through tight lips, "Tomorrow, you go out."

I looked at him again and said, "Sir, you must be kidding."

A muscle in his jaw tensed and twitched. He was trying hard to control himself as he said, "Hold out your hand." Puzzled, I did as he ordered.

He took a key from his desk and slapped it into my hand. "Go into my personal storage room, and get your belongings. Do it, now!"

I went in and found my bundle. Opening it, I realized that they really were my personal effects and street clothing. I brought it back out and set it on the corner of his desk. Calling in one of his personal assistants, he ordered him, "Take these pants and shirt, and make sure that they are washed and ironed for tomorrow morning." That's all I heard before I was ushered back to my cell.

As the guards led me back down the hall through my cellblock, all the prisoners were calling out, "What happened? Did something happen to your family?"

Head spinning, I replied, "I don't know, I don't know. The superintendent said that I'm being released tomorrow."

The shouts came back, "Man, you're crazy! You're mad! You know you're in here for a long, long time! You're a hard-core addict, dude! They're not going to let you out! They're just messin' with you, man."

Back in my room, I drove all thoughts of release from my mind. I knew the others were right. As a hard-core addict, I could have been in there for several years. Besides, whenever anyone was released, the family knew a month in advance. There was a lot of paper work and procedures that had to be completed first. I knew my family would have told me if I was to be released. So, I convinced myself that this was the biggest joke in town. I figured they were just using some new way to break me by giving me hope and then tearing it away. I was determined not to hope; they'd only use it against me. I just went to bed as usual.

The next morning, I wasn't even awake yet when the prison guard came in, saying in Malay, *Bangun! Angkat Barang-Barang!* "Get up, let's go! Get all your belongings and let's go."

Scrambling from the bed, I didn't even pack. I just grabbed whatever I could and rushed out the door after the guard to the superintendent's office. I must have looked ridiculous standing there with my arms full of my bunched up belongings.

The superintendent just pointed to my neatly piled clothes and told me to change. They were starched and pressed to perfection. I signed my release forms and then was handed my ID card. As I stared down at my plastic ticket to freedom, the realization washed over me: this was the last day of my 'six-month bargain' with God. God had answered my prayer. All I could think was. "Wow!" My mind couldn't really comprehend what was happening.

The gates rolled open, and I found myself in the outside world. Right in front of my eyes, cars were whizzing by on the highway. Behind me, the guard chuckled as I took in the sights. *Pergi! Pergi!* "Go! Go! Don't eat our food anymore! Get out of here!" I wasn't about to give him time to have second thoughts. I went.

Before long, I was standing in front of the church: the Willoughby's house. I rang the bell and stood there looking into the yard through the iron gate. It seemed like I waited a long time before the bell was answered. As soon as the Willoughbys saw me, shock registered on their faces. They carefully approached the gate but didn't open it yet. They thought I had escaped from prison and letting me in would have put them and their work in jeopardy.

Bro. Willoughby looked puzzled as he asked, "What are you doing here? We just saw you two days ago in the chapel service, and you didn't say that you were being released!"

I was as confused as he was, but finally, I showed him my ID, and he was satisfied enough to open the gate.

Sitting there at their dining room table, they asked me what my intentions were, now that I'd been released. Without a moment's hesitation, I told them that I wanted to work at the church. As soon as I said that, I could see their eyes open wide as they gave each other sidelong glances. They were actually praying for someone to work in the church, but they had seen too many people come out of prison with the same request and then disappear, missing in action after a few days. So with obvious doubts but not wanting to discourage me, they said, "Sure. Come back on Monday morning, and you can start."

It was only Thursday. I was concerned about being unoccupied for the weekend, so said, "Well tomorrow is Friday, why don't I come then?" They assured me that Monday was soon enough. I would just have to live with their decision.

16

FREE TO WORK

That Sunday, I attended my first church service at one of the local hotels. It was a small group, and the people were all very warm and friendly. No one seemed to care that they were shaking hands and talking to an ex-convict and drug addict. I began to wonder if they even knew about my past. That afternoon, over lunch, Genny asked me what I wanted to do. I could tell she wasn't really expecting me to show up to work at the church the next morning. Was I a joker like some of the others that came this way or was I serious?

Indeed, I was serious. On Monday morning at 8 a.m., I was standing in front of the Willoughby's gate insistently ringing the doorbell. Bro. Willoughby came down with his hair all mussed. Obviously, my presence was unexpected at this hour. As if he didn't recognize me right away, he just said, "Well, can I help you?"

"I'm here to work," I replied.

"Oh, OK," he said and brought me in. I waited on the sofa while he got ready, and I watched their two children, Meghan and Barak, playing.

A few minutes later, looking much more collected, Bro. Willoughby called me into his office and asked, "So, what can you do? Can you type on the computer? Do you have any computer experience?"

"No," I said. "I have never touched a computer."

"Well, then what can you do?"

I hadn't really thought about it, and I was left fishing. "Well, I can photocopy, I can sweep the floor, I can clean the toilets."

He shook his head at the latter suggestions. "We don't want you to do that! You can photocopy." Then he stepped outside, and I heard him whispering with Sis. Willoughby in the hall, trying to decide what to do with me. I waited.

Finally, Sis. Willoughby came in and dropped a two-foot stack of books in front of me. She went through them, pointing to each, "Three copies of this, two copies of that, six copies of this here." These were books on marriage counseling, Exploring God's Word, and Bible correspondence. The subject matter was very different from anything I had ever read. I went to work.

I finished the first day at 5 p.m. – that was the deal. I would work from 8 a.m. to 5 p.m. with an hour break for lunch. Working silently, I only replied when they talked to me. I was doing three things at once: photocopying, data entering, and duplicating tapes. It must have looked like a juggling act.

By the second day, the photocopier broke down because it was in constant motion. For some strange reason, eight hours of straight photocopying burned the machine out. Luckily, they had a deal to repair and service the photocopier. We would be seeing a lot of that repairman for the next while.

As soon as the machine was ready again, I went right back to work. Suddenly, from the doorway behind me, Sis. Willoughby screamed over the din of the various machines, "STOP WORK!"

Still photocopying, I thought this lady had gone crazy! I turned my head and saw her standing there with her hands on her hips.

"Stop work!" she repeated.

I didn't say anything; I was just thinking, "Why? It's not time to stop yet." She pulled me by the sleeve out into the kitchen and asked me what I wanted to eat. All the while I was saying, "No, no, no. I don't want anything."

She pressed me, "Would you like a cheese sandwich?"

"No, no, no," I said again. At the time, I didn't eat cheese, beef, or the likes. That was western food, and I was not familiar with these tastes. Before I knew it, Sis. Willoughby was working at the stove – buttering bread, slapping on thick cheese slices, and frying it up. She then plopped the plate down in front of me and watched to see if I would eat it. I gave that sandwich a leery look and forced a half-hearted smile as I picked it up and nibbled a little bit off the corner.

Just then, Bro. Willoughby walked in saying, "Oh, you're having a grilled cheese sandwich! Good."

I was nibbling and hoping desperately that they would just go away so I could throw it out, but he was urging me on and joking with me to try and get me to eat it. Relenting, I took a bite and started chewing. To my surprise, I actually liked it.

Sis. Willoughby was really putting her foot down now. "You have one hour to rest. Don't go back in the office when you finish eating. Take a one-hour rest."

However, in less than an hour, I was back in the office working away again. She came in, "No, you're supposed to take a rest!" What was I going to do with an hour break? I had just finished spending so many months being idle. I was happy to be occupied.

"But I don't have anything else to do," I insisted. "Just let me work!" I just wanted to finish the job.

After about a month, Genny and the Willoughbys called me out to the dining room. The three of them were lined up across from me as they prepared to lay down the law. They told me firmly, "We're going to pay you five dollars a day."

"No, I don't want money. I just want to work," I insisted. "If you're going to give me money, I don't want to work." They were looking at each other like I was crazy, but for the time being, they let me have my way.

By the third month, they called me in again. This time, they gave me an ultimatum. They had checked with the Ministry of Labor and had found out that they were liable if I was not paid. They were serious and said, "If you don't take money, you can't work here anymore."

So I bargained with them, "Why don't you give me three dollars a day? That's enough to cover my transportation."

114

They wouldn't budge. "No way, we've decided to pay you five dollars a day. Take it or leave it. Now, how do you want us to pay you?"

"Just pay me daily," I replied.

They didn't give up. "No, we want to pay you once a month." I refused. "Well, we'll pay you weekly then," they said.

That wasn't too bad. The thought running through my mind was that I didn't want extra money in my hands to buy drugs. I was serious about wanting to change. I knew that this time it was a matter of life and death.

It got even worse. The next month, in spite of my protests, they increased my salary to ten dollars a day. If I couldn't control whether they paid me or not, I was determined to work as hard as possible for them in return. I worked five and a half days a week, as well as transporting and setting up musical equipment for our Sunday services.

About four months after my release, Rev. Billy Cole came to Singapore to preach our very first crusade. A week before his arrival, I was found to have a one-inch kidney stone. It was quite a serious case. I was hospitalized for three days while they ran tests and x-rays, and it was decided that they would have to laser-blast the stone.

However, during our Saturday afternoon service, God took care of any procedure I may have needed.

Rev. Cole was preaching, and I was videotaping the service. All the while, I was fighting excruciating pain. Suddenly, right in the middle of preaching, Rev. Cole looked up at me and called me down to the altar. "We want to pray for you," he said.

As he prayed for me, I felt the anointing of the Holy Ghost, and I knew that God was healing my body. After that service, the pain gradually subsided, and by the time I went for my treatment they couldn't locate the stone.

I was sitting in the doctor's office waiting for my test results when the doctor entered. He was holding my folder and wearing a puzzled look on his face. "Did you pass your kidney stone?" he asked.

As if I could pass a one inch stone! I told him I hadn't.

"Well, did you take the medication I gave you to break down the stone?"

At this point I had to make a confession, "No, to tell you the truth, I mixed that drink up the first time and tried it, but it was so nasty I just couldn't drink anymore." There in the office, I let him know that man's medicine hadn't done it. God healed me! I was living proof of Psalm 103:3, *"Who forgiveth all thine iniquities; who healeth all thy diseases."*

The work at the church continued, and we were growing nicely. With all these new people and outreach opportunities, we were outgrowing our accounting and filing system. I decided that I could probably reorganize things and started bookkeeping and entering the data into the computer. By that time, I was an expert at two-finger typing.

As I worked on the accounts, I realized that the income of the church was very minimal. Genny and the Willoughbys must have been paying my wages out of their own pockets. Their personal sacrifice touched my heart, and I determined to work even harder. I also received many blessings from others in the church. They slipped me a little extra cash here and there and even bought clothing for me. Everyone was so generous. Not only were they concerned about my spiritual well-being, but they also took care of every daily need.

As the church grew and more people started to pay tithes and offerings, we were able to take on two more staff members to help with the workload. This extra help allowed me to take on some new responsibilities. I began to encourage some of the newer people, and I also began to work with other ex-addicts who had just been released from prison. Whoever would have thought? All my life I had always been on the receiving end of counseling, and here I was helping others get their lives straightened out. Unbelievable! I was aware of the fact that, for the first time in my life, I had a true purpose and meaning.

There came a point when we were outgrowing again. This time, it was the Willoughby's home. We needed larger facilities to manage the church affairs, so we rented a big three-story, six-room bungalow. It was perfect for our needs. This became our administrative office as well as our fellowship and prayer meeting center. Genny and our Filipino pastor and his wife took up residence here as well. This new space was put to full use.

At the same time, we rented the worship hall at the hotel for the full day, instead of just the morning slot. We were having two services every Sunday. The local congregation met in the morning, and the Filipino congregation met in the afternoon. With God's blessing, and under the loving care of the

Willoughbys and Genny, the church began to sprout and grow. These were exciting times.

In the very beginning, Genny was the key person that God used to develop the church. She loved these people, and she showed it in many ways. Not only did she give of herself and her time in ministry, she also gave of her own finances to meet the needs of the church, often down to her last cent.

People would often give her money to treat herself or provide for her needs, but immediately it would be in one hand and out the other hand to take care of someone else's need. On questioning her and telling her that she had to stop this and look out for herself, she replied, "When God stops giving, I'll stop giving."

She was especially burdened for the ex-addicts that had just been released from the prison. I followed her around like a shadow, observing her unique ways of dealing with people and situations. Working with Genny impacted me deeply, causing me to develop a similar desire to be a soul winner. She sacrificed so much without even having a second thought for her own personal gain. She was my mentor. Life was good. Never in my wildest dreams did I think that I'd be associated with such people and be on their side.

While Genny was very instrumental in starting the work in Singapore, she would be the first to say that she was not the pastor that the church needed.

Rev. Steve and Sis. Barb Willoughby were in Malaysia at the time and would often travel back and forth to Singapore to assist Genny. Their original intention was not to move to Singapore, but God had other plans. I believe they were hand-picked for this awesome responsibility. They were the perfect couple to fulfill this role. They were full of wisdom and sensitivity. Together, they teamed up to be a mighty force in the Kingdom of God, and the church continued to grow in leaps and bounds. The local people loved them.

The Willoughbys also had a great impact on my life. They were a dynamic couple and had faith to move mountains. They believed that God could move the mountains in my life, and so, I believed it too. If they were wary of me in those early months, they didn't show it. All they showed instead was love and acceptance.

A month after I was released from prison, I was baptized in Jesus Name. As Bro. Willoughby and I waded out into the hotel swimming pool, I felt anxious to go down into the water because I was still feeling dirty inside. As I gripped Bro. Willoughby's wrist, he spoke over me, "Xenn Seah, upon the confession of your faith and by the authority of the Word of God, I now baptize you in the name of the Lord Jesus Christ for the remission of your sins!"

With the final word, he plunged me backward, fully immersing me in the waters of baptism and raising me up again. As I came up streaming water, hands flung in the air, I felt release like never before. It was as if a huge weight had rolled off my back and had sunk to the bottom of the pool. I felt clean, free, liberated!

At the time, I didn't completely understand that baptism was for the remission of my sins. I didn't know all the theology and how it all worked, but I believed that if I took that step, God would do the rest. Because of my willingness, God continued to give me an understanding of the deeper meaning of its significance.

After my baptism, everything changed. I didn't know it then, but as I walked out of the pool, I was walking differently. As Romans 6:4 says, *"Therefore we are buried with him by baptism into death: that like as Christ was raised up from the dead by the glory of the Father, even so we also should walk in newness of life."* My dedication to that newness of life was soon to be tested.

I was determined to keep my repentance fresh, as Singapore is a small place, and it is hard for an ex-addict to get away from the drug subculture that exists. It lurks in every residential area and every coffee shop. It's especially hard if you've been in gangs or have sworn oaths and allegiances to societies. Maybe you had debt from moneylenders before being arrested, and they're now on your case for you to push until you've paid what you owe. In any case, so-called 'friends' and foe keep tabs on you, and they know when you are discharged.

It took only days for me to be contacted by someone trying to pull me back to where I had come from. I still knew where to score and who had the good stuff. I knew where to get a few straws full of drugs to get by, and I knew where the moneylenders were. There just didn't seem to be anywhere to hide, so I had to stand firm and learn to overcome by the grace of God.

One Monday afternoon, I was on my way to the bank to deposit the offering money from the Sunday services. As I approached the bank, an old buddy of mine was suddenly by my side. He leaned in close and whispered, "I've got some good stuff with me right now. Come on over, you can have some."

Right away, I changed the subject and tried to talk about anything other than the drugs. I could feel the pull. A voice inside was screaming at me to take the money, buy the drugs, and let things go back to normal. But, I fought it down. After chatting briefly, he took out a slip of paper and a pencil and quickly jotted something down. He slipped it into my hand saying, "Here's my pager number; call me if you want anything." Then he was gone.

All the way to the bank, I kept my hand clenched tight around that scrap of paper, never looking at it. I just knew the number would burn itself into my brain if I even glanced at it. The temptation was so strong.

When I got back to the house, my fist was still closed around the number. I walked through the house from one room to the next, winding my way to the washroom. There I paused a moment; closed-hand poised over the toilet. Temptation and dedication warred back and forth within me in that second, and then the Spirit prompted me, "You don't need that. I've got something much more satisfying for you." My hand snapped open, and the sweaty ball of paper fell while I flushed. Instantly, a wave of release washed over me.

After that incident, I had boldness when talking to my old friends. Whenever they'd offer me anything, I'd politely refuse and start telling them about how God changed me and set me free. They usually left me alone pretty quickly.

Through it all, I learned that even in the greatest trials and temptations, God will never leave me or forsake me. Just as His Word promised, with every temptation, He made a way of escape so I would be able to bear it. I learned the secret of James 4:7, *"Submit yourselves therefore to God. Resist the devil, and he will flee from you."* First submission, then resistance. Still, I had to be willing to forge ahead and resist temptations, especially in discouraging times. As I Peter 5:7-8 states, *"Casting all your care upon him; for he careth for you. Be sober, be vigilant; because your adversary the devil, as a roaring lion, walketh about, seeking whom he may devour."* God gave me strength in times of emotional distress, replacing the drugs I once relied on with His peace and joy.

Yet, even with all this progress, months after my baptism, I still hadn't received the Holy Ghost. I was still resisting it. There were a lot of people that received the Holy Ghost all around me, but I don't know why it didn't get into my head. Even when people were praying for me, I refused to receive it.

Six months after my release, in November 1992, Bro. Frank Tamel, from Parkway Apostolic Church, came for the first time to minister during a Holy Ghost Crusade. When the altar call was given, I busied myself around the back, finding things to do so I wouldn't have to go up to the front. I was legitimately occupied, On the other hand, I was trying to avoid having people pray for me and being put on the spot to receive the Holy Ghost.

I could see Bro. Tamel at the front, praying people through to the Holy Ghost. Soon, he was coming down the aisle toward me. I tried to slip away, but he cornered me and said, "I'm going to pray for you, and you're going to receive the Holy

Ghost." True enough, I received the baptism of the Holy Ghost that very day.

I began speaking in tongues; in a language I didn't understand. It flowed so naturally. It was like nothing I'd ever experienced before. It was a revelation. Pure joy! I was flying on the highest high ever. It all happened just as I'd read in the book of Acts 2:4, *"And they were all filled with the Holy Ghost, and began to speak with other tongues, as the Spirit gave them utterance."*

After I received the Holy Ghost, my walk with God began to gradually improve. I began to seriously think about my spiritual life. There was so much garbage in my head because of my past, but the Holy Ghost helped me to delete it. He began to prompt me, giving me a renewed understanding of right and wrong, and why certain things weren't beneficial for me.

Receiving the Holy Ghost changed me. As it says in Ephesians 4:23, *"And be renewed in the spirit of your mind."* This was the turning point in my spiritual life. My personal "Cross Over" from darkness to light.

17

TRIP TO AMERICA

A month later, I approached Genny and told her that I wanted to go to America. To be specific, I wanted to go to Parkway Apostolic Church in Oak Creek, Wisconsin. This was Genny's home church, and the Tamels were pastoring there. I felt safe and accepted in their midst and felt that this was a good place to learn more about administration as well as expand my understanding of serving people.

In reply, Genny just looked at me and smiled. I knew that in the back of her head she was thinking that it was impossible for me to leave the country. I was still under probation, and gaining a visa to America at that time would be very difficult. She didn't say a word, so I dropped the subject for the time being.

I brought it up with her about two weeks later. This time, she told me that if it was going to happen, we would have to pray and fast.

About a week later, I approached her again and she simply replied, "OK, we have to get a few things in order first. You have to get your passport."

I became doubtful. I had to request permission from the police to apply for my passport, and I knew it would be pretty much hopeless. They don't just hand out international passports to ex-prisoners on probation and supervision.

Amazingly, we submitted the necessary papers, and in return, they granted me permission to apply. This very rarely happened. When we received this news, we were so excited and thankful that God had allowed this miracle. Now, the second obstacle was getting a visa.

At the time, the US immigration was very strict about giving visas to anyone with criminal or drug records. Once again, our only hope was God. We knew that if it were His will, it would happen. We prayed and sent in the application. The usual waiting time was three days for the embassy to respond to a visa application. By the third day, I was expecting every phone call to be them, but by the end of that day, I still hadn't heard a thing.

On the fourth day, they finally called and asked me to come down to the embassy. I walked through the doors of the embassy fully expecting to be rejected. I walked up to the counter and gave the attendant my name. She handed me my passport without a word. Leaving elated, I flipped open the booklet and got another surprise. The embassy had given me an indefinite, multiple-travel visa! I was shocked! It was a miracle.

I came back triumphantly with the passport and visa, and right away Genny asked, "Do you have money to go to America? How much do you have?"

I really hadn't thought about it. I'd been so focused on getting the paperwork in order, which seemed so impossible. I said, "No, I don't have any money."

With simple faith, she just replied, "Well, now we need to pray for the money."

It worked! God made a way! Philippians 4:19 says, *"But my God shall supply all your need according to his riches in glory by Christ Jesus."* I was provided with air tickets to America, and on top of that, someone gave me a thousand dollars US cash for spending while there.

Looking out the porthole window of the airplane as we circled in to land in Milwaukee, Wisconsin, I thought it was strange how everything was white. As we leveled out for landing, I realized that everything was blanketed in snow. It was February 1993, and a cold winter wind tossed wisps of snow across the tarmac, occasionally blowing up to touch my window. I was delighted! It was the first time I had ever seen snow.

As I walked out into the terminal, Bro. and Sis. Frank Tamel and Bro. and Sis. David Barnes came forward to welcome me. We headed for the parking lot in the subzero weather, and Bro. Barnes handed me a jacket. "Here. Put this on. It's cold out there," he said.

I had come without a jacket and was just wearing a sweater. I was reluctant to put it on because I was enjoying the cold air. Singapore is so hot and muggy, and this weather was a novelty for me. Finally, I put the jacket on. It felt like a weight and draped on me like a tent.

No sooner had we stepped outside when Bro. Barnes pelted me with a snowball, shouting "Welcome to America!" We all enjoyed a good laugh at my expense.

We arrived at Bro. Frank Tamel's home where I would be staying for the next three months. They showed me to my room. It was huge and had a walk-in closet as big as some of my living spaces during my prison days.

Sis. Tamel was very concerned about how to feed me, as I still didn't drink milk or eat beef or cheese. I came home that first evening and, right away, Sis. Tamel asked, "What would you like to eat?"

As guests, the Chinese people don't demand anything, so I just said, "Whatever is convenient."

The next thing I knew, she plunked down a sizzling hamburger, loaded thick with cheese. It was like the grilled cheese sandwich all over again. Against all my misgivings, I took a tentative bite and started to chew in order to be polite. My eyes lit up and I exclaimed, "Oh wow, this is good. I've been missing out!" We had McDonalds in Singapore, but I would only eat their fish sandwich. During my stay, I began to enjoy a lot of Western food.

The next day, Bro. Frank Tamel took me to the church and put me to work. We knew my time there was limited. I was in awe as I looked around, and I realized that this was not a little church I was coming to!

Bro. Frank Tamel and his son Bro. Anthony Tamel worked hand in hand to make sure everything ran smoothly and efficiently. Bro. Anthony Tamel had a gift for administration that really appealed to me. He realized that as things progressed and the church grew, a proper foundation had to be in place in order to be organized and effective. I liked his way of thinking.

The administrative building, the sanctuary, the school – there was so much to take in. From Monday to Friday, I went to the church and observed how they functioned. Everything ran like clockwork.

Bro. Frank Tamel assigned me to different sections and departments where I would work for a week at a time, going through the administration, the accounting, the bookstore, and even the maintenance of the church. I had an opportunity to sit in on the Christian school. I really enjoyed this, as the children peppered me with questions about Singapore.

I absorbed so much throughout my stay. I covered so many aspects of how a church runs, not only in theory but in practice as well. Even during the services, my eyes were opened wide as I observed how things were conducted. During this whole time, everyone received me with open arms.

A week before I was to go home, I had mixed feelings because I had grown to love and respect the Tamels. They were like a mother and a father to me. They treated me so well and had invited me into their lives. I was overwhelmed with the love they showed me. Never in the past had I been treated this way. When the day came for me to leave, it was a struggle for me to get onto the plane. After three months in Parkway, I returned home and immediately started implementing what I had learned.

18

DREAMS

She was a dream. At least that's how I first saw her. In my dream, she was walking towards me in the airport where I was standing with Rosalind and Morten, a couple from our church. I didn't know quite what to make of the dream until a few days later when Rosalind told me that she and her husband were picking up an AIMer (Associate in Missions) at the airport. She was stationed in Indonesia and working under Pastor and Sis. White, Missionaries to Indonesia, and was coming to Singapore to renew her visa.

I said, "I know, I've seen her." Rosalind looked at me strangely – obviously puzzled. Mischievously, I said no more and let her wonder.

Without knowing any of this, Genny asked me to accompany them to pick up this lady from my dreams. She gave me a name – Barb. Riding down to the airport on the bus, I managed to sit still and forced myself not to fidget, but I was excited and nervous because of my dream.

Standing there in the terminal, we scanned the crowd looking for this AIMer we were supposed to pick up. Rosalind was looking for her friend, but I was looking for the woman I'd seen in my dreams. There she was, making her way through the milling throngs. I tapped Rosalind, "Rosalind do you see that lady in green? That is the lady that we are picking up."

She cast me an odd glance. "How did you know?"

"I told you, I've seen her before."

The two of us decided to play a trick on Barb. Rosalind was a tiny girl, and so, she hid behind me while I waved wildly to Barb. Although Barb spotted me waving, she didn't pay any attention to me. She was looking out for Rosalind. I waved again wildly. This continued a few more times, and Barb had a rather puzzled look on her face. Finally, Rosalind popped up and showed herself, waving Barb over. We all had a good laugh.

Later, Barb would say, "Well, I didn't know who that handsome man was, waving at me." Then she paused and said with a smile, "But I didn't mind."

It was December 1993, in the middle of Singapore's huge Christmas festival. The streets were lit up brilliantly. Genny was really busy at the time, so she asked me to show Barb around for the duration of her stay: a responsibility I was more than willing to accept. We went shopping and showed Barb the sights. She was good natured and easy to be with. Her gentle spirit attracted me.

As we talked, I quickly realized that she was the one – or at least I wanted her to be the one! The hand of God was once again at work in my life. How else do you explain two people from opposite ends of the world coming together?

Not only were we from opposite ends of the world, but our lives were totally opposite as well. She was stunned when I began to share my story with her: how God had saved me from the pits of hell and how He placed my feet on a firm foundation. She couldn't believe her ears, and I began to wonder if I was revealing too much, too soon. Later, she was to tell me that I was the kind of person that she would have walked across the street from if we would have crossed paths in the past.

No sooner was Barb in Singapore when she had to return to Indonesia. We visited back and forth a few times, and then she returned to Canada. She was on my mind constantly. Could it ever be possible that such a woman would grace my life?

We both had to know where this was going, so I visited her in Canada for a period of time and then decided to continue our romance through long distance phone calls. We certainly did our part to keep the phone companies in business that year.

Finally, I proposed, and to my joy, she accepted. We were married in Canada in 1995 and then went back to Singapore to continue working in the ministry. Barb was a dream come true. A 'helpmeet' in every sense of the word. She was involved in many areas of the work, especially in teaching Bible Studies and in ministering to the ladies. She was a real blessing, and the people loved her. Of course, she was a blessing to me too, to have her at my side and in my life.

Our first child, Scott, was born in Singapore in 1997. Once again, I was overwhelmed with God's goodness to me. When I looked into his little face, so vulnerable and trusting, I was determined to do all I could to make sure that his life was spared from the scene I grew up in. I wanted him to know that God's love is unconditional and so was mine.

19

A HIGHER PURPOSE

In 1999, my family and I embarked on a new adventure: we moved to Canada. Our original thinking was that we would set up a business, become self-supporting, and go back to Singapore to continue with the ministry. Funny how our plans are not always God's plans!

We started a restaurant in Ottawa, Ontario, called "The Singapore Noodle." It was a hard job, a disaster from the beginning or so it seemed at the time. Barb was at home with Scott and our brand new baby, Erin, trying to balance books that were constantly in the red. I was at the restaurant from morning till night. My day off was Sunday, but I was basically no good for anything. I was exhausted and didn't have energy for either my family or my church.

My mother came to live with us for a year to offer us her assistance. She gave every ounce of energy she had to help us in our endeavor. She spent her days along side of me in the restaurant and then came home to help out where she could with two busy children. She also was exhausted. After the first year, we realized that this just wasn't going to work.

We desperately wanted to sell the restaurant, but we couldn't even find a buyer. We were bound to a lease, and we were going from bad to worse, fast.

This was a horrible time in our lives. Everything looked bleak. Little did we know, that through this disaster, God would finally turn everything around and create something beautiful out of the confusion. As our personal dream collapsed, God started to open up a far greater cause. We prayed and fasted, and many of our church family in Stittsville, a suburb of Ottawa, also prayed and fasted with us. It didn't take long for God to open a new door of opportunity for us. He truly made "a way in the sea, and a path in the mighty waters."

During these dark days of ours, God was laying the foundation for our new direction. Most of our restaurant kitchen staff were Chinese people from Mainland China. In talking with them, we soon realized that we weren't the only ones who had struggles and needs. These people's stories really touched our heart. They were all highly educated professionals, sweating it out in minimal wage jobs.

The education system in China is so intense, that only the very top scorers would ever really have much of a chance at success there. These parents basically gave up their own futures for their children futures. Living far from family and friends and anything familiar to them, they were willing to give up everything so that their children would have a better life with better opportunities in Canada.

These people thought they were coming to a land of milk and honey, but they were in for a big surprise when they actually arrived in Canada. The hi-tech industry was on its way to collapse, and the language barrier was enormous. Jobs and opportunities were scarce. Imagine engineers, university professors, and editors now slinging noodles. We saw such need in their lives. If anything, just a local friend to guide them through the maze of a foreign land would be helpful.

One morning, while my staff and I were preparing the food for our lunch buffet, I felt a heavy burden, and I knew that God was impressing a plan of action on my heart. It was actually while I was frying a batch of noodles in a big sizzling wok that the Lord spoke to me and said, "Why don't you teach them phonics lessons using the Bible?" Wow! What a great idea!

I went home that night and shared my thoughts with Barb. She was equally as excited and felt the burden as well.

Barb was already familiar with an approach for teaching English. She had taught phonics with Sis. Willoughby, and she also taught "English as a Second Language" in a Language School in Singapore. She knew that she had a system that worked.

When I approached my staff about our offer, they were ecstatic. This was just what they needed. The fact that these classes were free of charge was an added bonus to them. Everybody likes a freebie!

We met in one of their homes, and our first class began with a bang. There were six students in attendance, with the promise of more the next week.

They were the ones receiving instruction, but Barb and I were having a great time too. It became a much-needed diversion for us, as it helped us take our minds off our own struggles. I think that there is a principle involved here: as we reach out to meet the needs of others, God will take care of meeting our needs!

It's a well-known fact that laughter is good for the soul, and laugh, we did! It turned out that these precious people had a wide range of English skills. Some knew how to read and write and had a good understanding of the language, but their pronunciation was in the bottom of their socks. Others only understood a few words. We all laughed as they tried to roll their tongue around the new sounds they were learning. The end result was that they all improved greatly and were beginning to gain more confidence in speaking with the local people.

These English skills were especially important for some of the Chinese men. Some were fortunate enough to have secured jobs in their fields of study but were hindered from feeling like they were accepted because of their lack of proper pronunciation. Now, instead of hearing nothing but, "Pardon me? Pardon me?" and constantly being asked to repeat themselves, they were being understood and began to feel more comfortable in their environment.

We started to meet many other Chinese people in Ottawa who were jobless and in need of English skills and cultural understanding. We bonded many of them and extended our hands to them in any way we could.

Finally, after coming very close to losing everything – house included – we breathed a huge sigh of relief as we found a buyer for the restaurant. Then, the Chinese ministry really began to blossom!

Of course, we realized that God was bringing these Chinese people into our lives not only to teach them English and to be a friend, but also to introduce them to Jesus: a friend who sticks closer than a brother, a friend whom we can cast all our cares upon, because He cares for us.

After twelve weeks of phonics lessons, the next phase of study was "English Comprehension", through the avenue of a twelve-week Bible Study. Initially, we didn't know if they would be interested in this approach, but they loved it. We were obviously opening up their minds to a whole new realm about which they had no idea. They were familiar with Bible stories but were not aware that they held spiritual content. Their curiosity and hunger were obvious.

As more and more people came into the phonics classes and Bible studies, we realized that we needed to be more organized and come up with a bigger plan, so we decided to start a Chinese service.

By this time, Pastor Dummitt and the rest of our local congregation were well aware of what was taking place and were fully supportive. Many were already involved in Bible Studies with some of the Chinese people. In fact, Pastor Dummitt and the local congregation graciously extended themselves to help to support my family financially so that I would be able to concentrate on developing this ministry further.

Pastors Frank and Anthony Tamel and their assembly have also been very gracious in helping to support this ministry financially. Not only did they support financially, but I had also spent many hours on the phone with them, being encouraged and advised on how to develop this endeavor.

After getting together with Pastor Dummitt to discuss the situation, we came up with a plan of action. Since we already had a morning and an evening service on Sundays, the only available time slot for a Chinese service was in the afternoon.

It was decided. We would offer phonics classes at 2 p.m. and then meet in the sanctuary at 3 p.m. for a church service. We approached the Chinese people with our plan and they were excited. We would teach them basic phonics, and in order to practice and improve their language skills, they would communicate and interact with local people.

As this ministry was opening up, the vast majority of our local congregation began to get involved, and the burden to help the Chinese people spread. Many volunteered their time and energy to teach phonics classes and Bible studies. Far beyond the in-church activities, people from opposite ends of the world were quickly becoming friends with each other. Both sides were learning about each other's traditions and culture. It was, and is, a great learning experience for all.

Within the past year, of those who we have been in contact with, nine have been baptized in Jesus name and fifteen have already received the Holy Ghost. They are finding new life in Jesus Christ and are growing in grace every day.

These people come from an atheistic background. China is a communist country that attempts to be void of all religion. There are deep mindsets and traditions that need to be replaced with the truth and reality of Jesus Christ. But nothing is impossible with Jesus. It's happening right in front of our eyes.

Romans 8:38-39 states, *"For I am persuaded, that neither death, nor life, nor angels, nor principalities, nor powers, nor things present, nor things to come. Nor height, nor depth, nor any other creature, shall be able to separate us from the love of God, which is in Christ Jesus our Lord."* God has His ways of dealing with us right where we are, no matter who we are, and it has been a joy to see these precious people also make a "Cross Over."

We have met some truly amazing people and have been blessed many times over with the privilege of their friendship.

We are all in this together. We are here to walk with our Chinese brothers and sisters, and we watch in wonder as Jesus reveals Himself to them more and more. One day we will all "Cross Over" into eternity, and every tear, every hardship, every trial will have been worth it all when we look into the face of our Lord and Savior, Jesus Christ!

This story does not end here. As in the Ottawa area, there are Chinese people all over the world who are looking for meaning in their lives. Like every one of us, they too are looking for something that will satisfy the longing of their souls.

Recently, I had the privilege of preaching at the Third National Chinese Conference in Los Angeles, California. I was overwhelmed by what I witnessed. Many Chinese people came from all over the countryside in search of a deeper experience in Jesus. They may have had an experience with this Jesus, but they knew that they were still missing something. They needed "power" to change their lives and be effective. They needed the "born again" experience.

As these people humbled themselves and opened their hearts to the Word of God, God filled them with the Holy Ghost, and they began to speak with other tongues as the Spirit gave them utterance. Some have already been baptized in Jesus Name, and all are looking forward to growing in Christ!

Jesus is alive and well, and it is a privilege to be a part of God's Kingdom!

Some words from our Chinese friends:

Terry Huang: I met Mr. Seah in April 2001. One of my friends told me about a job in his restaurant. I applied because I really needed this job to help support my family. I worked with Mr. Seah in the kitchen, and he impressed me as being a man of honesty and integrity. Mr. Seah likes to help other people, and when he knew that our Chinese people were having a big problem in speaking English, he and his wife, Barbara, were very patient to teach us proper English pronunciation. This was very helpful.

Then he started to talk to us about the Bible: about what the standard of a good person is according to the Bible. I didn't believe the Bible when he first talked about it because in China we don't believe Jesus. I had many doubts and didn't believe that God existed. But as Mr. Seah began to tell us about his own past and how he also did not believe Jesus, I started to feel differently. If Jesus could help Mr. Seah and do this in his life, then maybe Jesus did exist. Soon, Jesus started to touch my heart and show me that He was real in my life, and I know that He loves me and can help me with my problems.

I have been baptized in Jesus name, and I have the Holy Ghost. My husband and my friend also have the Holy Ghost. I am happy now.

George Gong: I came from China to study at Carleton University. My family is paying a lot of money for my education and it's important that I do well. However, my English was not very good, and I had to pass an English course in order to continue to study for my degree.

I was introduced to Mr. Seah through a friend of mine so that I could study English. Mr. Seah's wife was my teacher, and she helped me to pronounce English words better. Also, many of the youth in the church have become my friends and they have helped me with my communication skills.

Besides the English study, I was also introduced to God and His word. Our system in China is a communist system, and when I lived there I didn't know about God. I depended on Chinese cultures and traditions. I got through life on my own wit and intellect. I have very strong opinions, and it is hard for someone to change my mind about something.

I am a good person and always believe it is important to be a good person. Buddha's teachings are like this.

I've studied the Bible for seven months now, and I saw many common beliefs found in China. Jesus and Buddha both teach that you should be a good person, but one big difference, I realize, is that

Jesus can help you and change things in your life but Buddha cannot.

Even though I don't know God very well yet, or understand the Bible very well, I can say that the Bible relates to many situations I find myself in, and it offers many solutions. I can say that I have not found anything wrong. I agree that truth is truth. There cannot be ten different truths. I am reading the Bible with an open heart, and I am very encouraged and excited by it.

Before, I used to feel like God was on the 12th floor and I was on the 1st floor. Now I feel like I'm close to God, like I can touch God. I feel that I'm getting to know God more and more and that I can connect with Him quickly when I pray and when I worship Him.

I have repented of my sins, have been baptized in Jesus Name, and have received the Holy Ghost. My heart is quiet now.

Mr. Seah and the church encourage me and support me. They have become my family. I will continue to go this way!

20

CONCLUSION

After coming from a Buddhist background and being out on the street unaware of a loving God for so many years, knowing Him was a totally new experience. I have found that the relationship I have developed with Him is very real. It has been the most amazing experience of my life.

My dad never tucked me into bed; he never told me that he loved me; I never got a hug from him. But, from the moment I stepped into that little prison chapel, my Heavenly Father wrapped his loving arms around me and drew me close. God's love and the love of God's people surrounded me and poured over me.

I had never felt such a thing before. This kind of response overwhelmed me. I felt safe and secure for the first time in my life. I felt like I finally belonged somewhere. People I didn't even know were willing to accept me and welcome me into their lives. The genuine spirit of God's people was shown by the fact that they didn't even consider my past. Such a man as I!

I am sure you are intrigued with many of the things I've revealed about my life, my many ups and

145

downs, struggles, and victories. After I got out, did I struggle with temptation? Yes. Did I struggle with relationships? Yes. Did I struggle with vices and bad habits? Yes. Did I struggle with rebuilding my life? Yes. Did I struggle to find a place in society and the body of Christ? Yes. But struggle and victory are what being an "overcomer" is all about. I John 5:4 reads, *"For whatsoever is born of God overcometh the world: and this is the victory that overcometh the world, even our faith."*

"Overcoming" doesn't just happen. I still strive for it and sometimes even struggle for it. I pray, I cry, and I determine in my heart that through the cross of Christ, I will "Cross Over" and have the victory. And so, looking back and looking forward, I echo Paul's words in I Corinthians 15:57, *"But thanks be to God, which giveth us the victory through our Lord Jesus Christ."*

Writing this book was difficult because it seemed to be a book without a hero: there was very little that was heroic about my life. But there is a hero – Jesus. Those of you, like me, whose lives have been shipwrecked, know assuredly that He will rescue you just as he rescued me. He is no respecter of persons. Jesus loves you and wants you to know the Gospel because it is the power of God unto salvation. He knows you, and you can know Him too: on a personal level, not just in theory.

If you have never experienced the transforming power of God as I have, why don't you give yourself a chance? God is standing at the door of your heart, and He is knocking. If you open yourself up to Him, He will begin to reveal Himself to you. If you've tried everything else that this life has to offer and still feel that something is missing, try Jesus. You will find that only He can truly satisfy.

Barb and I were blessed with a second child in May 2000. Erin Ashley Rei came into our lives, and she is a bundle of joy. Again, I was made aware of the awesome responsibility I have to walk right with Jesus. Most definitely, my children are watching me and in one way or another, they will pattern their lives after my example. I want them to see Jesus in me. At three years old, Erin is aware of Jesus. As I see her sing her songs and raise her little hands in worship, I am determined to keep my experience fresh and live an overcoming life.

Two weeks after his sixth birthday, my son, Scott, received the Holy Ghost. The next day, shaking under the power of God's Spirit, he helped pray two of his young friends, Ryan and Rachel, through to the Holy Ghost as well. The following Sunday, I was privileged to baptize my six-year-old son in the name of Jesus. As he went down in the water, I felt a thrill. At his age, I was already in the opium dens with my grandfather.

My children's lives still lie before them, lives that are so precious and filled with opportunity, rather than being bound for ruin like the traumatic ,life I led. Because I allowed God to transform my life, my children's heritage is now a heavenly one instead of one bound for hell. And so, I beg you, don't wait until your life is half spent before coming to God, as I did. Have faith like a little child, and God will blow you away!

TESTIMONIES

The stark austerity of a Singapore prison is sobering, to say the least. You are kept healthy with a clean environment, forced parade style exercise, and a boring, mundane diet, but there is absolutely no effort made for your physical comfort and very little for your mental comfort. In Singapore, 2 degrees north of the equator, there are no air-conditioned cells, no mattress on your bed because there is no bed, no screens on the windows to keep the mosquitoes at bay, no TV privileges, and no library. In fact, if you think of anything you would hope to have during a period of incarceration, more than likely it doesn't exist in a Singapore prison.

Being but a speck of land among the continents, Singapore says they have but one natural resource, and that is brainpower. With their brainpower, they have soared from third world to, "front of the line", first world in less than thirty years. No one has ever succeeded at success like Singapore. Consequently, a brain clouded and befuddled by drugs is a big liability in this high pressure, hi-tech environment of success at all cost.

The prisons are graded according to first, second, or third timers. By the time you arrive at a third timer prison, your expiration date for success has long expired, leaving you in the shambles of utter scorn and contempt by a society that just can't tolerate your failure. You've had three strikes, you're out, you are considered beyond help. The commandant of one of the prisons once told me, "It is hopeless. We might as well put a revolving door at the release gate because they will all be back." If the man responsible for your "rehabilitation" has no hope, then you are hopeless. As unredeemable, who cares how you feel or what you think? Why put much help or hope into the hopeless? You will just be disappointed because they never change.

Everybody else has given up, so most of the inmates have also thrown in the towel. They live in a cruel vice of excitement and dread of their release date. They are excited to taste, smell, and see the outside world again, but tortured with the statistical reality of an almost inevitable return to prison life. In most minds, it is not if I come back, but when.

Still, the system goes through the motions. A little bit of religious counseling is allowed. It was in this world of rejection, despondency, and depression that I met a man called Xenn.

I liked having Xenn in the Bible study class. It was a large class. Really too large, giving it the potential to get a little chaotic and unruly if not handled carefully. I was not so naive to think that all were there to learn about Jesus. Still, my awareness and "radar" capabilities were infantile compared to the deceit and nonsense these experienced con men could manufacture. So, I always needed help. I needed someone that at least thought I was sincere enough to deserve a little respect. The right ally could help me keep a lid on things but not so tight that it would stifle their desire to be there. Xenn filled the bill. He was calm, attentive, and respectful. I didn't know what he was thinking on the inside or if he was buying into any of it at first, but on the outside, he gave the appearance of listening. It also didn't hurt that he cast quite an imposing physical shadow across the classroom. He was twice as big as most, and his bulk wasn't from fat. I noticed that when order was asked for, his compliance and sweeping glances seemed to bring calm to the thirty or so restless natives.

It is hard to get close or personal with thirty men in a two hour, once a week counseling session. I was a fish that knew nothing about their water. I had never been in their world of addiction and sorrow. I could not pretend to relate to or understand what they were going through from any personal experience. But I had something that was in short supply in that world. I had hope. I had faith: not in any rehabilitation program but in a transformation experience. In Xenn's world of crushing hopelessness, I held out Jesus as the one and only solution. He thought he had heard, seen and done it all, but here was a new story previously untold. I wasn't skillful in my presentation, but I was sincere. It was enough to keep Xenn coming back week after week. I'm not sure at this point how much Xenn actually believed or understood. I think he probably thought that it was all too good to be true. But he couldn't escape the hound of hope and so he found himself wanting to believe and receive help from this Jesus of Nazareth. Little by little, this story of amazing grace, love, and mercy from the man Christ Jesus, started penetrating walls that were much more foreboding and excluding than the locks and bars of his physical prison. Walls of despair and dejection, walls of shame and disgrace, began to melt under the love of Jesus.

It was obvious that Jesus was having an impact on Xenn's life. He showed it by his classroom faithfulness and participation. A bigger indicator was his response to songs and worship. It takes a strong commitment to overcome prison peer pressure and be a worshiper. Xenn was my ideal student.

Then one day, Xenn acted totally out of character. I was bringing the group to order, taking attendance, and getting them seated on the floor. Two or three times I gave a general invitation for all to be seated; all of which Xenn ignored. I was just about to get tough and issue a strong rebuke when the thought occurred to me that Xenn had never disobeyed me before. Therefore, it stood to reason there must be good cause for his quiet defiance. Suddenly it struck me. The only reason he wouldn't sit is if he couldn't sit. That left only one conclusion. He must have received his caning sentence. If that was true, then his only crime was not a case of insubordination but of extraordinary commitment. I let him stand the whole two hours. The wisdom of that decision was not revealed until months later when my suspicion was confirmed. That act of human will and choice will stand, for my entire life, as one of earth's most powerful testimonies. I will never forget that Jesus can become such a strong attraction that even the horrendous pain of having your buttocks flayed by caning will not deter or prevent you from his presence.

Still, with all this, I was surprised at the intensity of Xenn's determination and the extent he would go to turn his life around after his release. A man with a history of bad decisions started to, by the wisdom and word of God, make all the right decisions. He severed his association with his past, which is no mean feat in tiny Singapore where your extensive past can bump into you on any corner.

We desperately needed help with the daily managerial and administrative matters of the growing church, but we had almost nothing to offer in wages. I believe we were an answer to each other's prayers. We needed willing hands to do any and everything they could find to do, from sweeping to sending visitor letters. He needed a safe haven of love and trust, an environment of acceptance and approval. Before it was all over, the ex-addict and ex-con Xenn Seah, would handle tens of thousands of dollars, with multiplied thousands at his disposal. During stints of deputation, he managed my financial affairs in Singapore, as well as always being at the forefront of Tabernacle of Joy affairs. He has the love and respect of every saint and member who has known him. He selflessly poured himself into the body of Christ like few I know. No one has ever had a higher level of trust from me. I did and do trust him with my very life. Some have questioned the wisdom of giving such far-ranging trust and confidence to a man with such a sordid past. It really wasn't hard. When Jesus is in the picture, I am an eternal optimist. Jesus has power to transform. Xenn was and is one of the most phenomenal examples of that power I have ever known.

It is no surprise to me that Xenn has moved into a new arena, a new dimension of being used by God. It won't be his last.

May thousands of thousands of souls, especially Chinese, come to know the Savior through your life and devotion, is my prayer. May you live in fullness and fruitfulness all the days of your life, Xenn Seah.

Your friend forever,

Steve Willoughby

My name is Genny Miller. I originally worked as an AIMer (Associate in Missions) in Greece and Malaysia, and then lived in Singapore for a number of years. With the blessing of the Starks, the current missionaries at the time, I started a local endeavor, which later became Tabernacle of Joy, Singapore.

In order to substantiate my visa to live in Singapore, I accepted a job as a Drug Counsellor for drug addicts. While working for the Singapore Anti-Narcotics Association (SANA), I went into the Drug Rehabilitation Centers (DRCs) of Singapore to conduct counseling sessions and teach Bible studies. This is where Xenn Seah and I first crossed paths.

When I first met Xenn, years ago, he was not yet the overcomer you see today, free from the guilt of the past and from his fears of tomorrow. He was in and out of prison and the drug culture in Singapore for many years. Actually, he was in more than one prison, but he didn't even know it.

Upon his release from prison, he truly had a humble start. He worked in the church office, in the Willoughby's home, doing odd jobs and a lot of photocopying. He was determined to stay away from the things of this world and be near the things of God. He recognized that this was imperative to his survival.

Xenn truly is an exemplary model of a life that was laden with sin and darkness but is now filled with truth and light. Not only does he have the victory, but he is making a difference for those around him, as well. It hasn't always been easy, but the battles he has won have helped him to make the "Cross Over" in this life, and one day it will be those same battles that will help Xenn make the eternal "Cross Over".

Not all of the ex-drug addicts do well after they are released. You see, even when one repents, is baptized, and receives the Holy Ghost as Xenn did, coming out and trying to survive in a brand new way isn't easy. People shun you, many jobs won't accept you, and many times family members may even avoid you, as you are viewed as problematic. It can be a big adjustment for everyone.

I say all of this so you can really understand the victory Xenn beams with in his life. He cherishes what the Lord has done for him and is determined to keep moving forward and take as many with him as he can along the way. He knows the meaning of I Peter 2:9-10, *"But ye are a chosen generation, a royal priesthood, an holy nation, a peculiar people; that ye should shew forth the praises of him who hath called you out of darkness into his marvelous light. Which in time past were not a people, but are now the people of God: which had not obtained mercy, but now have obtained mercy."*

As God was investing in Xenn, he was growing from a baby Christian, coming from a Buddhist background to a mature Christian that God could entrust things to. He became a "Jack of all Trades" for Tabernacle of Joy, doing everything from photocopying to purchasing materials, organizing functions, and praise singing. He worked hard and diligently, yet for a very small wage.

His very humble beginning was part of a growth process that is still going on today. I am sure he struggled with pride, lack of funds, and peer pressure, but he resisted and prevailed. He has gained the love and respect of all those in Tabernacle of Joy.

Xenn was especially effective in our "Overcomers Ministry". This is a program that is geared towards helping struggling ex-addicts change their ways. He learned to teach Bible Studies, and he also visited and worked with other drug dependents and their troubled families. Since he had a similar background and could understand where they were coming from, he was an encouragement to these families and a ray of hope for many a wife who suffered and found it hard to believe that their husbands could change someday.

As the church was growing, Xenn was elevated to the position of Chief Administrator and ultimately Zone Pastor. He began to wade into deeper waters in Christ.

As he grew into these duties he was always dependable and trustworthy. He proved himself to be very capable. The Willoughbys or I could pass any job to Xenn, and we could count on him to get it done and get it done well.

Many of these duties were new to him, and they didn't come without pressure, but he never complained. He didn't count the long hours and days spent counseling, teaching, or visiting. During many of these busy, trying days, especially when the Willoughbys were back in America for a year on deputation, Xenn was like my right arm. He thinks I was his mentor, but I learned many things from working closely with him, as well. From being his counselor, sister, pastor, friend, and co-worker, I have seen his life – and many others because of him – pass over many barriers into victory. I am not over praising Xenn. If you know him, you know what I mean.

Xenn knew "how to talk", and he was always able to get fair prices for us. I believe he saved Tabernacle of Joy a lot of money because he had God's favor upon him.

Since we didn't have our own facility for some time, we had to haul, set up, and tear down the equipment before and after every service. Most often, it was Xenn and other ex-addicts who did this work. And it was work! It was a thankless and unnoticed job, but God noticed Xenn and every other brother who contributed in that ministry. Good servants grow up to be good leaders. If you cannot serve – you cannot lead.

These were hard working days for Xenn but happy ones serving the Lord. These were years of development and preparation for what lay ahead – like Moses.

There are other "overcomers" like Xenn, still worshipping at Tabernacle of Joy, of whom I am equally proud and close to. But there are many who failed to strive, and they succumbed to temptations. They let their guard down and went astray. I've heard about some of Xenn's old buddies who were arrested again and again, or who died in fights. Many overdosed or committed suicide. When things like this happen, they can shatter one's faith and shake those of like background to realize that it could have been them. There were so many heartbreaking times. This could have been Xenn. Yet through it all, Xenn determined to pray more, draw from the power of the Holy Ghost, and dedicate himself to work harder for God.

It was a thrill to watch Xenn's life and ministry unfold. He has a desire to excel in any area he puts his hand to. I watched as he ventured to North America: to Parkway Apostolic Church in Oak Creek, Wisconsin. His purpose was to receive training in Church Administration and in serving people.

I watched as a Canadian girl, Barbara, came into Xenn's life and stole his heart. They fell in love and later married. It was beautiful to see.

After a few years of living in Singapore and being a blessing to the work of God, they felt to move to Canada. I was with them in encouragement and prayer as they opened up a restaurant, only to have it drain them of all energy and resources.

Xenn had many dreams and plans that have been shattered, one by one, since he has been in Canada. He had worked hard, yet failed; almost losing everything. It seemed he'd lost out on his dream. This, however, was just another time to overcome and walk in God's grace and mercy.

It didn't take long for God to open up a new direction for Xenn and Barb. Now, with the restaurant behind him and much loss, God is showing them both why they are really in Canada.

God has opened a door for Xenn and Barb. Xenn is now a licensed Minister of the Gospel. He and his wife team up with a system to teach English and impart Bible understanding to the Chinese people in their community. Not only to help the Chinese learn English but befriend and help them culturally and spiritually as well. Some are being baptized and filled with the Holy Ghost, speaking with tongues as the Spirit enables them. They too, enjoy a new found life in Jesus Christ because Xenn and Barb are extending themselves in love and sacrifice.

Together, they have developed a system that would be a blessing to any church. It is only in the beginning stages and in the process. I believe God will continue to open new windows of heaven to Xenn and Barb as they put their hands to the plough for the Gospel of Jesus Christ to reach the Chinese. Xenn is willing to cross over once again, like Abraham, to a land that he knows not; but he does know that God is the builder and maker of it.

Many today, are focusing on China but don't know what to do. You don't have to go overseas to minister to these people. Just look in your own communities and neighborhoods. Many Chinese have already left their homeland, and they are just as empty here as they were there. They need someone right here who can help them know Jesus.

Xenn is a people person. He likes to talk. He has a way with people, and he knows truth. He is willing to extend himself and is not afraid of hard work. God wants to use this sort of person.

Is this the end of Xenn's story? No. He is still on the potter's wheel. There may be more times of affliction and scars, but Xenn is letting God change him, develop him, and use him to reach out to the Chinese people for His kingdom.

It is a blessing that he would even write this book to share with you what God has done for him and what God can do with you if you are willing. If God can take a man like Xenn and change him, bless him, and use him for His Kingdom, how much more you? You who don't have a drug background, you with a high education, you who never were in prison, you who never lost your business, resources, and dreams in this life? You have resources, education, and time. God is looking for you to make yourself available. There is so much to do. I believe God weeps over the lost and perishing and weeps over our slothfulness and indifference when He has given us so much. Stop spinning your wheels. The harvest is ripe and the laborers are few. Listen to the voice of God... He just may have a plan for you!

We, who have been born-again, have experienced the power of God that changes lives, breaks habits, and overcomes obstacles. We know Jesus, the living God who heals and forgives and saves. We have a message that can break bondages and set people free from demon powers. We have the Holy Ghost and gifts of the Spirit actively working in our lives. We have the privilege of knowing and using the name of Jesus to bring power and resources from the heavenly realm into the problems and circumstances of everyday life.

We have the answer, and we need to live it and prove it to a world that doesn't understand what we have. The cross of Jesus Christ has transformed our lives, which were once filled with scars. We know the Savior and Creator of all. We walk in the power and might of the Holy Ghost. We must tell the world around us of what Jesus has done. What He did for us, He can do for others, too. Jesus is no respecter of persons. He is real, and He's coming soon.

It has been my joy to work with Xenn and see him change and grow. I trust, you too, will have been encouraged by reading how God transformed someone from the rubbles of ruin into a powerful, humble man of God who truly has crossed over and intends to move ahead by the leading of God's Spirit.

Dr. Genny Miller

Xenn is a testimony for Jesus Christ and a witness to the power of change through God's presence in a life.

He has gone from a life of drugs, prison, selfishness, and serving Satan, to a life of freedom and serving God and His kingdom. He has a powerful anointing upon his life and ministry, while maintaining a spirit of humility and submission to the guidance of leadership.

He and his wife, Barbara, have been a real blessing to the Stittsville Church. When Xenn's restaurant business was sold and no job opportunities were available, the church in Stittsville readily responded to help meet their financial need so he could develop the Chinese ministry and outreach.

The church is very excited and happy to be involved in the Chinese outreach.

He will continue to be mightily used of God, and we have yet to see God use him in an even greater way.

Rev. Alonzo Dummitt

48108048R00098

Made in the USA
San Bernardino, CA
20 August 2019